TWAYNE'S WORLD AUTHORS SERIES

A Survey of the World's Literature

GERMANY

Ulrich Weisstein, Indiana University

EDITOR

Wilhelm Busch

TWAS 525

Wilhelm Busch

WILHELM BUSCH

By DIETER P. LOTZE
Allegheny College

TWAYNE PUBLISHERS
A DIVISION OF G. K. HALL & CO., BOSTON

Printed on permanent/durable acid-free paper and bound
in the United States of America

First Printing

Library of Congress Cataloging in Publication Data

Lotze, Dieter P
Wilhelm Busch.

(Twayne's world authors series ; TWAS 525 : Germany)
1. Busch, Wilhelm, 1832-1908—Criticism and interpretation.
PT2603.U8Z725   831'.8   78-14843
ISBN 0-8057-6365-1

For Barbara

About the Author

Dieter P. Lotze was born in Hanover, Germany, in 1933. After the Gymnasium in Celle, he studied German and English philology and literatures as well as comparative literature at West Berlin's Free University and at Innsbruck University where he received his doctorate with a dissertation on German-Hungarian literary relations. He began his teaching career in the United States in 1961 as Instructor in Modern Languages at Allegheny College where he is presently holding a position as Professor of Modern Languages. He also taught as Visiting Professor of German at Colorado College. He became a naturalized citizen in 1967. His special research interests are nineteenth century literature in Germany and Hungary, comparative studies, and the methodology of language instruction. His articles on pedagogy and on literature (Busch, Celan, Heine, Victor Hugo, Kafka, Lessing, Madách) have appeared in publications in the United States, Germany, Hungary, and Japan. He is presently working on a monograph on Imre Madách for the Hungarian section of Twayne's World Authors Series.

Preface

Wilhelm Busch started his autobiographical sketch of 1894 with a thought about appearance and reality: "Nothing looks the way it is. Least of all man, this leather bag full of tricks and dodges." This warning should be kept in mind when surveying the work of the man who tried to provide insights into this "leather bag," and who continues to be dismissed by much of his audience as a harmless entertainer. His special place in the cultural landscape of the nineteenth century is only gradually being recognized.

Since this is the first critical study of Wilhelm Busch in English, it seemed advisable to deal with all significant facets of his literary oeuvre rather than to discuss selected aspects of it in depth. The focus is on Busch as a writer; a detailed analysis of his accomplishments as a painter and graphic artist would have gone beyond the scope of this book. Yet, he told his stories in pictures as well as in words, and I am grateful to the publishers for agreeing to include some illustrations as examples of the author's successful blend of text and drawing. The picture story is Busch's unique creation, and the relative emphasis on it in this study—without neglecting his poetry and prose writings— also reflects this genre's quantitative predominance in his work.

Except where noted, I have used my own literal translations. No attempt has been made to reproduce Busch's rhyme or meter in English. For most of the verse quotations and some of the prose passages, the original text is also given so that readers familiar with German may have some idea of Busch's style and can test the accuracy of Albert Einstein's observation: "Wilhelm Busch, especially Busch the writer, is one of the greatest masters of stylistic precision. I think—except, perhaps, for Lichtenberg—there has not been his equal in the German language."[1] Quotations cited in the text simply by volume and page numbers refer to the critical edition of Busch's works by Friedrich Bohne, *Gesamtausgabe* (Hamburg: Standard-Verlag, 1959). Quotations from Busch's letters are taken from Bohne's edition, *Sämtliche Briefe* (Hanover: Wilhelm Busch Gesellschaft, 1968–69). The abbreviation "B" precedes volume and page numbers in these citations.

Contents

WILHELM BUSCH

My work on this book was made possible by a sabbatical leave and some financial aid granted me by Allegheny College. I owe thanks to many persons. Rudolph Wiemann's permission to quote from his translations of *Schnurrdiburr oder die Bienen* (*The Bees*) and *Fipps der Affe* (*Chip the Monkey*) is gratefully acknowledged. I am much obliged to Vera Crispin and Marjorie Rhinesmith who aided substantially in the preparation of the manuscript. I would like to thank Ulrich Weisstein, editor of the German section of Twayne's World Authors Series, for his many valuable suggestions. Special thanks go to the Wilhelm Busch Gesellschaft (Wilhelm Busch Society) in Hanover, Germany, and particularly to its executive director, Friedrich Bohne, who helped and encouraged me in many ways, who read the first draft of my manuscript, and who was instrumental in the preparation of the illustrations. Lastly, I would like to express my appreciation to my wife Barbara for her help and her willingness to become a Busch widow for the period of my work on this study.

DIETER P. LOTZE

Allegheny College

Chronology

1874 *Dideldum* (Tralira), *Kritik des Herzens* (Critique of the Heart).
1875 *Abenteuer eines Junggesellen* (A Bachelor's Adventures). Correspondence with Maria Anderson.
1876 *Herr und Frau Knopp* (Mr. and Mrs. Knopp).
1877 *Julchen* (Little Julie). Disagreement with Johanna Kessler. Acquaintance with Paul Lindau.
1878 *Die Haarbeutel* (Hair Bags). Article on Busch by Lindau.
1879 *Fipps der Affe* (*Chip the Monkey*).
1880 *Stippstörchen für Äuglein und Öhrchen* (Small Tales for Little Eyes and Little Ears). Friendship with Hermann Levi.
1882 *Plisch und Plum* (Plish and Plash).
1883 *Balduin Bählamm, der verhinderte Dichter* (Baldwin Baalamb, Poet Manqué).
1884 *Maler Klecksel* (Blotty the Painter).
1886 Eduard Daelen's *Über Wilhelm Busch und seine Bedeutung* (On Wilhelm Busch and His Significance). "Was mich betrifft" (As Far as I Am Concerned) as Busch's response.
1891 *Eduards Traum* (Edward's Dream). Reconciliation with Johanna Kessler.
1894 "Von mir über mich" (By Me About Me).
1895 *Der Schmetterling* (The Butterfly). Begins active correspondence with Grete Meyer.
1898 Busch moves to Mechtshausen.
1904 *Zu guter Letzt* (In the End).
1905 Manuscript for *Hernach* (Afterwards) is given to his nephew, Otto Nöldeke, for posthumous publication (published 1908).
1908 Busch dies on January 9.
1909 Posthumous collection of poetry, *Schein und Sein* (Appearance and Reality), published by Nöldeke.

CHAPTER 1

Busch's Life and Times

I *Three Quarters of a Century: 1832–1908*

MEIN Lebenslauf" (My Curriculum Vitae) is the title of a short poem by Wilhelm Busch, written less than a year before his death:

> Mein Lebenslauf ist bald erzählt.
> In stiller Ewigkeit verloren
> Schlief ich, und nichts hat mir gefehlt,
> Bis daß ich sichtbar ward geboren.
> Was aber nun?—Auf schwachen Krücken,
> Ein leichtes Bündel auf dem Rücken,
> Bin ich getrost dahingestolpert,
> Mitunter grad, mitunter krumm,
> Und schließlich mußt ich mich verschnaufen.
> Bedenklich rieb ich meine Glatze
> Und sah mich in der Gegend um.
> O weh! Ich war im Kreis gelaufen,
> Stand wiederum am alten Platze,
> Und vor mir dehnt sich lang und breit
> Wie ehedem, die Ewigkeit.

(My life is easy to relate. / I was asleep in peace eternal, / Not missing anything at all / Until I visibly was born into this world. / But then, what?—On feeble crutches, / A lightweight bundle on my back, / I've been stumbling on with confidence, / Sometimes a straight course, sometimes crooked, / And finally I had to catch my breath. / I scratched my bald head contemplatively / And took a look around me. / Alas! I had run in a circle, / And found myself in the old spot once again, / And there, before me, vast and wide, / Just as it did previously, stretches eternity.) (4.536)

What is depicted here as a circular course leading from eternity to

eternity translates into seventy-five years of a rich and creative life
that spans the period from 1832, the year of Goethe's death, to 1908,
the year when Franz Kafka published his first prose pieces. Busch's
literary work shows tendencies which can be found in both authors.
In 1832 Busch's native village of Wiedensahl was part of the
Kingdom of Hanover, and it was in the capital of that country that he
experienced the revolution of 1848 as a college student. As a mature
man, Busch saw his native region become a province of Prussia and
later of the new German Reich created by Bismarck. He observed the
unprecedented economic boom of the years following the Franco-
Prussian War. He watched the emergence of the working class as a
political force attempting to realize the demands of Marx's *Communist Manifesto*, and the Chancellor's attempts to deal with the
Socialists as well as with the Catholic church's role in German
politics.

The political and economic changes that Busch was to witness in his
lifetime were largely conditioned by technological developments.
Machines were revolutionizing industrial production and transportation. When nine-year-old Wilhelm moved from Wiedensahl to
Ebergötzen to be educated by his mother's brother, the journey took
three days by horse-drawn cart. When he frequently repeated the
trip in later years to visit his friend Bachmann, rail transportation had
reduced travel time to a few hours. And at seventy-two, he wrote his
niece Grete Meyer: "My visit to Frankfort stood under the sign of the
automobile. Hundreds of those stinkers rushed back and forth, and in
doing so, blared, I imagine, like rhinoceroses in the jungle. At first,
these things strike you as uncanny, and yet they may well be the land
vehicles of the future. Coaches, drawn by horses—these poor
grasshoppers—really look quite antiquated by comparison" (B,
2.224).

In this whimsical description, Wilhelm Busch emerges rather
clearly: the man who called himself "a pessimist for the present, but
an optimist for the future" (B, 1.139) had observed enough change to
realize its inevitability, albeit with some regret. He was a realist who
could not quite overcome his longing for a more romantic past.
Essentially a man of the nineteenth century, he had a chance to cast a
glance at the beginning of a new age, marked by the insights of
Sigmund Freud and Albert Einstein. Despite long periods of urban
residence, he had remained what he was at the start of his "curriculum vitae," a son of rural North Germany.

II *The Formative Years*

In the 1830s, the village of Wiedensahl was similar to many farming communities in the North German plains. Johann Friedrich Wilhelm Busch and his wife Henriette Dorothee Charlotte, née Kleine, owned and managed the general store. Busch's paternal ancestors were almost all farmers; on his mother's side we find peasants as well as barber-surgeons and soldiers. It is indicative of Friedrich Busch's individual drive as well as of the drastic changes in the social structure of the nineteenth century, allowing unprecedented upward mobility, that three of his five sons attended institutions of higher learning. Wilhelm, the oldest, was meant to become a mechanical engineer; Otto, who was to play an important role in his brother's life by introducing him to the Kessler family and by assisting him in his Schopenhauer studies, obtained a doctorate in philosophy and worked as a private tutor; Hermann, the youngest, studied mathematics and became a *Gymnasium* teacher. Busch's sister Fanny married a Lutheran minister.

Busch's literary portrait of his parents is limited to the barest essentials. In 1894 he wrote, "My father was a grocer, cheerful and willing to work; my mother, quiet and religious, was very busy in house and garden. The 'wings' of time have not been able to wipe from my grateful memory the love and also the discipline that I have received from them" (4.205). One of the reasons for the brevity of this rather sober statement may be Busch's hesitancy about sharing deep personal emotions with the general public. But the impression conveyed here is that of a highly controlled and cool home atmosphere.

By 1841, the Busch home had become too small for the growing family, and Wilhelm was sent to his uncle Georg Kleine, clergyman at Ebergötzen near Göttingen. Not until three years later would the child have an opportunity to visit his family again. Pastor Kleine must have been a remarkable man. His private tutoring enabled his nephew later to enter the Hanover Polytechnic College without the benefit of public education. Through him Busch was introduced to the world of literature, and his instruction in metrics was to pay off in later years when the budding author began to write poetry. His "approximate acquaintance" with the four fundamental operations of arithmetic turned out to be a sufficient basis for engineering studies. But the youngster was not only exposed to academic subjects. Kleine was a dedicated beekeeper and even edited a journal devoted to bees, and Wilhelm's exposure to the apiarian field was so thorough that at one point he contemplated a future as a beekeeper in Brazil. Young Busch was an avid reader. Reading fairy tales is listed as his favorite hobby for the period spent with his uncle, topping even activities like drawing, trout fishing, and bird catching. But weightier reading matter was devoured too: the local innkeeper made a collection of freethinking pamphlets available, and even Kant's philosophy was tackled. Erich Bachmann, whose father owned the water mill, became his closest friend and companion, and it is not hard to see Erich and Wilhelm as the original "naughty boys," Max and Moritz. Their friendship was to last until Bachmann's death. Up to that time, the Ebergötzen mill continued to be one of the author's favorite retreats.

The engineering studies in Hanover turned out to be a frustrating experience: "In pure mathematics I soared to a grade of 'A plus,' but in applied mathematics I moved with my wings flapping more and more weakly" (4.208). After struggling for more than three years, the drastic change in his career plans became clear: Busch left Hanover in order to become an artist. His disappointed father gave his consent, and the painter-to-be enrolled at the Düsseldorf Art Academy.

Busch worked diligently in Düsseldorf, but the general approach to art he encountered there was not to his liking. So he transferred to the Royal Academy in Antwerp, where he not only received excellent instruction but, more importantly, became acquainted with the masterpieces of Dutch and Flemish art. This experience was so overwhelming for him that he noted in his diary on June 26, 1852: "Let this day mark the more definite shaping of my character as a human being and as a painter. Let this be my second birthday."[1] But at the same time, the confrontation with the great art of the past, especially the paintings of Rubens, Brouwer, Teniers, and Frans Hals, resulted in lasting doubts as to his own artistic ability.

A severe case of typhoid fever, resulting in complete physical and psychological collapse, brought an end to his studies in Antwerp. During his convalescence in Wiedensahl and in Lüthorst, a village halfway between Göttingen and Hanover where Georg Kleine had assumed his ministerial duties, Busch started collecting folkloristic material: fairy tales, legends, and folk songs. An attempt to publish this collection, "Ut ôler welt" (From Ancient Days), illustrated with his own drawings, was unsuccessful. Busch himself soon realized that he lacked the proper background for a truly scholarly treatment of the haphazardly accumulated material. Sketching, studying biology (partly under Kleine's guidance), and reading—Schopenhauer and Darwin are prominently mentioned for this period[2]—kept him busy until he felt ready to resume his interrupted art education, this time at the Royal Academy of Art in Munich.

III *Years of Maturity*

With a population of approximately 95,000, Munich in the early 1850s was rapidly developing into a major cultural center, attracting painters and writers from many parts of Germany. Busch was intrigued by the city he called "die kunst- und bierberühmte Residenz" ("the capital city famous for its art and beer") (4.153), a phrase reminiscent of Heine's reference to Göttingen as being "famous for its sausages and its university." A busy social life began to engage him, especially in the artists' club Jung-München (Young Munich), which he joined during his first month in the metropolis. But the academy proved another disappointing experience: "My little Flemish boat, however, which probably was poorly steered as well, did not really get afloat in the academic current of that time. All the more pleasant was the artists' club where we sang and drank, and in addition used to tease each other through caricatures" (4.210).

The cartoons he contributed to the group's journal were to become very important. A frequent guest of the club was Kaspar Braun, who together with Friedrich Schneider had founded in 1844 a humorous and satirical weekly magazine *Fliegende Blätter* (Flying Leaves or Loose Leaves). Braun was impressed with Busch's graphic talent and sense of humor, and in 1858 invited him to become a regular contributor to his journal, and later to the *Münchener Bilderbogen* (Munich Picture Strips), started in 1859. The artist eagerly accepted, and for the first time in his life was financially independent of his family who had supported him for so long. From the humble beginnings as an illustrator of stories and jokes by others grew the genre that was to make Busch famous: the picture story in which drawing and text would complement each other.

From 1854 to 1869, Busch spent much of his time in Munich, but he continued to consider Wiedensahl his real home. It was there he created most of his pictorial narratives, and it was rural North Germany that provided the setting for many of the early works published by Braun, including *Max und Moritz*.

Busch's brother Otto had accepted a position as private tutor for the children of the wealthy banker J. D. H. Kessler and his wife Johanna in Frankfort. Wilhelm Busch's visit there in 1867 led to a lifelong friendship with Johanna who believed firmly in his artistic talent. Their cordial and stimulating relationship lasted until his death, interrupted only by a thirteen-year period of silence following a disagreement in 1877. Johanna's two daughters, Nanda and Letty, grew very fond of their "Uncle Wilhelm," and his letters to them, frequently in poetic form or decorated with his drawings, reveal a warm and charming correspondent. Busch moved his second residence from Munich to Frankfort for the next few years. The first chapter of *Die fromme Helene* (Pious Helena) presents a satirical description of the city.

Helene was the first of Busch's picture stories to be published by Otto Bassermann, a friend from the Jung-München days. Bassermann became his publisher in 1871, the year when the court ban on *Der heilige Antonius von Padua* (St. Anthony of Padua) was lifted. Otto Busch's book on Schopenhauer was also brought out by the young publisher, probably largely as a favor to his friend. Even though this treatise failed to shed any new light on the philosophy of the great pessimist, it is significant as the first attempt to link Wilhelm Busch's literary production to Schopenhauer. Otto used several quotations from his brother for illustrative purposes.

Other picture stories soon contributed to Busch's growing fame: *Pater Filucius*, an "allegorical tendentious piece," as his statement in the debate about the political role of the Catholic church in Germany; *Der Geburstag oder die Partikularisten* (The Birthday, or The Particularists), a humorous treatment of politics in a rural setting; the *Knopp* trilogy, a saga of bourgeois values and attitudes through two generations; *Fipps der Affe (Chip the Monkey)* and *Plisch und Plum* (Plish and Plash) as the continuation of the theme of mischievous animals that had started with "Hans Huckebein," the unfortunate raven; and finally the stories dealing with literature and art and the middle class, the fate of the would-be poet, *Balduin Bählamm* (Baldwin Baalamb), and the life story of *Maler Klecksel* (Blotty the Painter).

After 1872 Busch spent most of his time in Wiedensahl, maintaining no other residence. During his frequent visits to Munich, where friends had made a studio available to him, he always stayed at a hotel, even for extended periods. In 1881 he visited Munich for the last time. The man who had once been the moving spirit behind the festivities of the Munich artists' club, and who, among other things, had provided the librettos for light operas performed by his friends, turned more and more into the "Oansigl im Hinterwald" (Bavarian for "backwoods hermit"), as he jokingly referred to himself (B, 1. 249).

During the 1870s Busch formed a number of lasting friendships. Through the Munich artists' club Allotria (Tomfoolery) he met the painters Franz Lenbach and Friedrich Kaulbach, the architect Lorenz Gedon, and the conductor Hermann Levi. He became acquainted with Paul Lindau, who authored the first article dealing with Busch's work. Of particular interest is his extensive correspondence of 1875 with the Dutch writer Maria Anderson, prompted by her comments on his first volume of poetry, *Kritik des Herzens* (Critique of the Heart). In his letters to her, Busch revealed much about his personal world view. Some of the ideas presented here recur in his poetry and prose writings.

IV *The Final Years*

Had Busch truly "run in a circle"? From a geographic point of view, it would seem so. His path had led from a North German village by way of Düsseldorf, Antwerp, Munich, and Frankfort back to the relative seclusion of rural North Germany. In 1898 he and his widowed sister Fanny moved to Mechtshausen near the Harz Mountains. Busch's nephew Otto Nöldeke had taken over the Lutheran parish of that small community. The writer advised only his closest friends of the change in address; he increasingly resented intrusions upon his privacy. He said about himself: "With some justification, he could be called an eccentric. He is not very enthusiastic about company, except for that of one or two persons" (4. 211). He did not encourage visitors and usually suggested nearby towns as "neutral" territory for meetings with friends and acquaintances. In a letter to Kaulbach in 1888, Busch addressed himself to the question of his retreat, which must have puzzled many observers: "So the fellow sits in his corner and looks fairly satisfied. 'He does it out of principle,' says one. 'He does it out of necessity,' says another. 'He does it out of inclination,' says a third. The first laughs about him, the other pities him, the third feels contemptuous. Laughter, pity, contempt are, as to their root, close relatives, jointly arising out of the pleasant feeling of superiority" (B, 1. 294). But it would be wrong to equate privacy with isolation. Busch continued to maintain cordial relations with his friends, both through letters and through occasional reunions. In 1886, he accepted Lenbach's invitation to visit him in Rome. The multitude of new impressions was overwhelming, and Busch returned to Wiedensahl, happy to have seen so much beauty, but even happier to be home again. When, through Lenbach's mediation, a reconciliation with Johanna Kessler came about in 1891, Busch resumed his frequent visits to Frankfort.

His two major prose works of the 1890s, *Eduards Traum* (Edward's Dream) and *Der Schmetterling* (The Butterfly), must have been bewildering for an audience that saw in him mainly the creator of funny picture stories. Similarly, many readers failed to comprehend fully the message he was trying to convey in the last work he ever published, his collection of poems *Zu guter Letzt* (In the End). Later Otto Nöldeke would edit a posthumous volume of poetry that Busch may not have intended for publication, *Schein und Sein* (Appearance and Reality). Additional insights into his thinking can be gained from a number of aphorisms and notes found in his estate. Several of them represent the first versions of ideas which later grew into more formal lyrical statements. A final legacy was the manuscript for *Hernach* (Afterwards), a collection of drawings, sketches, and short poems that Busch gave to his nephew for posthumous publication.

Busch's lifelong interest in philosophy did not wane in his final years. Again, as in the case of Maria Anderson, he had a correspondent with whom he enjoyed sharing some of his insights. This time, several personal encounters could supplement what was written. (In the case of Mrs. Anderson, their first and only meeting had led to his rapid loss of interest in her.) The letters to his niece Grete Meyer show that he had remained under the spell of Schopenhauer, and that Nietzsche and his followers had failed to stir up any enthusiasm in him.

Toward the end of his life, Busch returned to one of his earliest interests, folkloristic studies. His concern with popular traditions, his desire to explore the possibilities of linguistic expression, and his familiarity with Plattdeutsch, the North German idiom that he had successfully incorporated into some of his works, led to intensive etymological investigations. He spent much of his last two days, after suffering a heart attack, reading in Kluge's etymological dictionary.

Death did not find Busch unprepared. For the anniversary edition of *Die fromme Helene*, published by Bassermann on the occasion of the author's seventy-fifth birthday, Busch had contributed a poem, "An Helene" (To Helena), in which he said:

Mir selbst ist so, als müßt ich bald verreisen
—Die Backenzähne schenkt ich schon den Mäusen—
Als müßt ich endlich mal den Ort verändern
Und weiter ziehn nach unbekannten Ländern.
Mein Bündel ist geschnürt. Ich geh zur See.
Und somit, Lenchen, sag ich Dir ade!

(I, myself, feel as if I had to go on a trip soon/ —My molars I have already donated to the mice—/ As if I finally had to change location/ And travel on to unknown lands./ My bundle is packed. I'll take to the sea./ And with that, Helen, I'm saying farewell to you!) (2. 544)

He was ready to depart for the "unknown lands," where so many of his close friends had preceded him: Gedon in 1883, Levi in 1900, Lenbach in 1904, and Bachmann in 1907. Two weeks before his death, he wrote his niece, whose first child had just died: "How sad that little Hildchen has left us already . . . What should I say? I am already standing at the border between here and there, and it almost seems to me as if both were the same" (B, 2. 273–74). On January 9, 1908, he crossed that border.

2.

3.

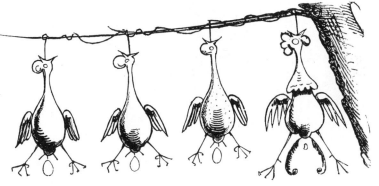

4.

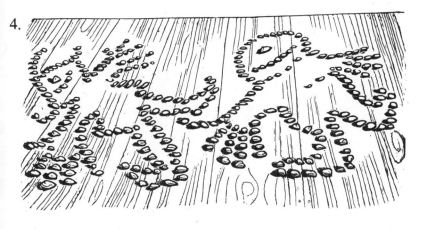

5.

6.

So ſtarben die drei ganz unverhofft.
O, Jüngling! da ſchau her!!!
So bringt ein einzig Mädchen oft
Drei Männer in's Malheur!!!!.

7.

8.

9.

10.

11.

12.

Ha! jetzt wird er
grausam heiter.
Er entdeckt die beiden
Streiter.

13.

14.

15.

16.

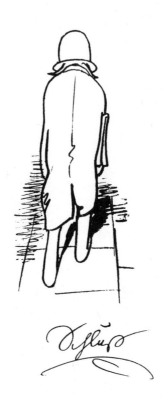

17.

18.

19.

20.

21.

22.

Comic Strip as Literature: Busch's Early Picture Stories

I   *The Beginnings: Flying Leaves and Picture Strips (1859–1864)*

IN his autobiographical sketch, Busch recalled: "It may have been in '59 when *Fliegende Blätter* received my first contribution: two men on the ice, one of whom loses his head. —I had to tell my tale on wood. . . . I, too, was interested in the interplay of desires, in growth and development. So, before long, the continuous picture stories began, which, as they almost automatically expanded over a period of time, met with more approval than their author could have expected" (4. 151). This "first contribution" was actually his fifth to be published in Braun's magazine. Even though this tale, for which the artist furnished both the text and a drawing, seems to have little in common with the masterpieces of his mature work, it is significant in several ways.

Busch's laconic summary does not do justice to "Der harte Winter" (The Severe Winter), this short narrative about two friends who go skating on an extremely cold day. One of them falls into a hole, and the sharp edge of the ice severs his head from his body. Due to the quick action of his companion and to the low temperature, the separated head can be reattached and freezes back into place. But as the two men are sitting by the warm stove in a tavern, a violent sneeze causes the unfortunate skater to lose his head again, this time permanently. Yet, the poor man does not despair. He finds a job carrying planks for a building contractor, and his lack of a head actually becomes an asset in his work.

Busch did not write this simple story specifically for the Munich periodical. It was part of the folkloristic material he had collected five years earlier. Thus, Busch's career as a humorist started with what rural North Germany had furnished him, rather than with a contribution from the lighthearted world of the Jung-München artists' club. It is no accident that the popular tradition of the fairy tale served as a stimulus. When, many years later, Busch was asked about the sources for his material, he responded: "Naturally, folk song, fairy tale, legend, have not gone silently past an almost perpetual villager like me. Some of that I have retold, the best I have kept for myself" (B, 1. 265–66).

"Der harte Winter" appears to start out like a conventional fairy tale: "Es war einmal ein unvernünftig kalter Winter; da gingen zwei gute Kameraden miteinander auf das Eis zum Schlitt-schuhlaufen" ("Once upon a time, there was an insensibly cold winter, when too good companions went ice skating together") (1. 12). Yet there are elements that seem alien to the genre: ice skating is not the kind of activity fairy tale heroes normally engage in, and Busch's linguistic treatment of the story adds an element of irony, since the adverbial modifier "insensibly" is rather unusual in this context. Similarly terms like "barbarische Kälte" ("barbaric cold") or "das war nun freilich für den armen Menschen recht fatal" ("this, however, was a rather calamitous situation for the poor man") do not quite fit the style of the folk tale. The very last sentence of the story is an elaborate pun, based on the colloquial idiom "ein Brett vor dem Kopf tragen" ("to have a board in front of one's head"), meaning "to be dense," or "to be a blockhead," which was becoming popular at the time when Busch jotted down the story: "Das war eine gar schöne, passende Arbeit für ihn, weil ihm dabei der Kopf niemals im Wege saß wie vielen anderen Leuten, die auch Bretter tragen müssen" ("That was a rather beautiful and fitting type of work for him, since in this way his head never interfered, as it does in the case of so many other people who also have to carry boards") (1. 13).

The lack of characterization ("two good companions"), and the emphasis on action are, of course, typical of the folk narrative, and decapitation with subsequent healing is a frequent motif in fairy tales. But the rationalistic explanations offered throughout (the hole in the ice as a result of ice fishing, the final separation of the head because of a sneeze that was the logical consequence of the fall into chilly water), and the realistic descriptive details (the unfortunate skater orders not just something to drink, but "bit-ters," and a "building contractor" provides him with a very specific kind of work) represent a different level of style and sophistication.

The fusion of heterogeneous elements (and the resulting impact

on readers or viewers) has frequently been seen as essential to the
definition of the *grotesque*: the technique Busch was to use so
many times in his works seems to make its first appearance in this
modest tale. We may be willing to accept the mysterious repair of
the physical damage as part of a fairy tale, but we are not prepared
to have it presented to us as a possible happening in our everyday
world. In this context, the illustration contributes further to the
intended alienation. Busch chose neither the accident nor the
unexpected happy ending for his drawing, but rather depicted the
two skaters as they are plodding through the high snow in heavy
wind. The innocuousness of the picture presents a striking contrast
to what is being related in the text. When Wolfgang Kayser sums
up the nature of the grotesque as "the estranged world"[1] and as "a
play with the absurd,"[2] his definitions could easily apply to this
first attempt by the young artist.

A comparison with Busch's later treatment of the perils of winter
shows technical refinement, but no significant change. His *Bilderpossen* (Antics in Pictures) of 1864 contains the picture story of
"Eispeter" ("Ice Peter"), which Kayser treats as an example of the
"realistic grotesque." Here the realistic element is initially emphasized even more strongly: the exceedingly cold winter occurred
in 1812, not just "once upon a time," and temperatures were so
low that frozen crows would fall off the trees, a fact presented in
verse and drawing. When young Peter sits down on a rock in order
to put his skates on, his pants freeze to the stone. An energetic
movement sets him free but also propels him into a hole in the ice.
Yet, as before, this is not the end of the unfortunate skater, who
manages to climb out again, but begins to sprout icicles until he
freezes to the ground looking like a porcupine. Things seem to
turn out well when he is found and taken home. Again, the warm
stove plays an apparently positive but ultimately destructive role:
the ice thaws, but, alas, the entire Peter melts away with it. All his
distressed parents can do is to spoon the steaming puddle into an
earthenware jar. The last picture shows a corner of the pantry.
Between a container labeled "Cheese" and a jar containing pickles,
there is, in somewhat elevated position, a big and tightly covered
cruse with Peter's name and three crosses on it (Ill. 1). The poor
skater is "preserved" here, who "after having been hard at the
beginning, later became soft as butter," as the accompanying text
explains (1. 303).

This is the final step in the change of a human being into an object, hinted at in the earlier story when a man was transformed into a plank-carrying device with no need for a head, and also suggested by the comparison of frozen Peter with a porcupine. The "play with the absurd" has become one of the characteristic aspects of Busch's work.

But we have to go back once more to the "estranged world" of the early prose tale. Busch described the decapitation scene as follows: "As the two skaters were going full steam, and inasmuch as the wind was blowing strongly, one of them made a mistake, slid into a hole and hit his neck so violently on the sharp edge of the ice that his head slithered along on the ice, and his body fell into the water" (1. 12). The unemotional report about the head "slithering" on the ice discourages any sympathy on the part of the reader, just as we cannot really feel sorry for a Peter who has become "soft as butter." The accident has severed the connection between the two component parts that used to constitute the whole of a person, and we can already suspect that the reunion of head and body, which have gone their separate ways, will only be temporary. Not only do we see the same objectification of a human being here as in "Ice Peter," but both stories depict man as having lost control over his environment. The skater has made a fatal mistake; now he is sliding, driven by the wind; a hole in the ice just happens to be in the path predetermined for him, not by him; and the cutting edge is exactly where his neck hits. Even in this first story we see an indication of a theme that will occur over and over in Busch's work, and that was most clearly expressed in Friedrich Theodor Vischer's 1879 novel, *Auch Einer* (Another One), as "die Tücke des Objekts," the "malice of the (inanimate) object."

Vischer's protagonist is fighting constant battles with the material world surrounding him. As he explains, all physics is actually metaphysics. The tendency, or even animosity, inherent in the objects, in the so-called "bodies," which traditional science labels with silly names like "law of gravity" or "statics," is actually the effect of the evil spirits that inhabit all objects: "From early dawn until late at night, as long as any human being is around, the object thinks of nothing but evil tricks, of malice . . . Every object, pencil, pen, inkwell, paper, cigar, glass, lamp—everything, everything is waiting for the moment when one does not pay attention."[3]

This is the world described by Busch, where puffs of wind, holes in the ice, and sharp edges are just waiting for a moment of inattention in order to cause the greatest possible damage. His picture stories are filled with malicious objects: pointed knives and sharp forks ready to pierce various parts of the human anatomy, watering cans and other vessels patiently standing in the appropriate spot until they can spill their contents over somebody, ovens and candles waiting in ambush for a person who could be burned, and many similar elements. Since Vischer was familiar with Busch's work, it is not impossible that the world view as proposed in *Auch Einer* owes something to the universe outlined in these picture stories. Both Vischer and Busch tried to employ laughter as a way to cope with the realization of the continuous threat posed by our hostile surroundings. Thus their works represent what Kayser arrived at as his final interpretation of the grotesque: "an attempt to invoke and subdue the demonic aspects of the world."[4] To be sure, Busch was not always able to subdue the demons he had invoked, but his much-debated "humor" represents the struggle to adjust to and rise above a world that is irrational and menacing. His popular poem about the trapped bird, starting to whistle a last merry tune as the hungry cat is approaching, has often been interpreted as his definition of humor, a view that is supported by Busch's laconic comment: "Der Vogel, scheint mir, hat Humor" ("The bird, it seems to me, has a sense of humor") (2.495). While this is no definition, it is significant as a statement about cheerfulness in view of the inevitability of doom. This ability to laugh despite everything sets Busch apart from his philosophical guide Schopenhauer, with whom he shared an essentially pessimistic outlook.

Otto Nöldeke relates a statement Busch made in connection with the art of Brouwer and Teniers: "Each object, even an earthenware pot, possesses a kind of sly hiddenness, which is overcome only by diligence, cunning, talent . . . It is difficult to find out nature's tricks."[5] Similar remarks show that this reference is not just to the skill required of an artist in copying nature, but to all matter as being alive and active—and as resisting all human attempts at control. He defined matter in one of his aphorisms as the "obstinacy of the smallest beings" (4.544), and he wrote to Lenbach: "I believe that in science, at which I cast an occasional glance, the dead foundation with which we have hitherto worked is gradually becoming alive. Friskiness, even on the smallest scale, would fit in nicely with the type of intellectual amusement I am accustomed to" (B, 2.64). "Obstinacy of the smallest living beings," "friskiness even on the smallest scale," and "sly hiddenness" all add up to Vischer's "malice of the object."

A few examples taken from Busch's early work for Braun must suffice here. In his first experiment with a picture story without words, "Die Maus oder Die gestörte Nachtruhe" (The Mouse, or The Night's Rest Interrupted) of 1860, the initial drawing shows in almost perfect symmetry two beds from which husband and wife peer at the little rodent on the floor that has obviously just interrupted their sleep. But the central position is reserved for a nightstand with a candlestick, a water bottle, and a glass. The arrangement is ominous, and sure enough, ten pictures later, the nightstand is toppling over, the bottle is broken, the water is splashing over the wife who has fallen to the floor, candle and candlestick have parted company, and the glass is falling and is about to hit the unfortunate woman.

In the humorous ballad, "Schreckliche Folgen eines Bleistiftes" (Horrible Consequences of a Pencil), the very title parodies the Romantic "ballads of fate" or "tragedies of fate," where usually some inanimate object plays a destructive role. In this case it is a "Pencil Number 7" which the budding artist Pedrillo, despite his teacher's admonitions, keeps sharpening on both ends. The "horrible consequences" occur when he embraces a pretty girl. But in contrast to the technique used in illustrating "Der harte Winter," this time the pictures tell the whole story: we see the two lovers pierced by a gigantic pencil. This use of exaggeration in order to emphasize the malicious object can also be found in many of the later picture stories.

Sharp or pointed objects are especially suited for destructive action. In "Der Bauer und der Windmüller" (The Peasant and the Windmiller), a saw is carried in such a way that one tooth cuts the nose of the nagging wife. Busch's phrasing is significant here: it is the malicious object that causes the damage, not the husband who carries the saw (even though his facial expression in the accompanying drawing leaves little doubt about the purposefulness of his action): "Ein Sägezahn trifft ganz genau / Ins Nasenloch der Bauersfrau. // Die Nase blutet fürchterlich, / Der Bauer denkt: 'Was kümmert's mich?' " ("A sawtooth hits exactly / The nostril of the peasant's wife. // The nose is bleeding frightfully, / The peasant thinks: 'What's that to me?' ") (1.127–28). Similarly, in "Diogenes und die bösen Buben von Korinth" (Diogenes and the Bad Boys of Corinth), two nails emerging from the barrel in which the philosopher had found refuge, become active and take revenge on the two boys who disturb the wise man's peace: "Zwei Nägel, die am Fasse stecken, / Fassen die Buben bei den Röcken" ("Two nails, sticking out from the barrel, / Grip the boys by their coats") (1.161).

"Die Rutschpartie" (The Sliding Party), published in 1864, provides perhaps the clearest example of the object taking over. Only at

the very beginning is the human being in control: "Da kommt der
Hans auf seinem Schlitten / Vergnügt den Berg herabgeritten"
("There comes Hans on his sled, / Merrily riding down the hill")
(1.274). The first victim of the malicious sled is the sexton who
happens to cross its path: "Schwupp! hat der Schlitten ihn gefaßt, /
Warum hat er nicht aufgepaßt?!" ("And presto! the sled caught hold of
him, / Why didn't he pay attention?") (1.275). Next come the hunter
and his dog:

> Schau, schau! Den Hund, den hat's bereits.
> Der Jäger spränge gern abseits;
> Jedoch der Schlitten faßt ihn schon,
> Die Tabakspfeife fliegt davon.

(Just look! The dog is caught already. / The hunter would like to jump aside; /
But the sled is seizing him this moment, / His tobacco pipe is flying off.)
(1.276)

The pipe has also developed a life of its own, it seems. The sled's
getting rid of its burden results in the discharge of the hunter's gun
through the sexton's hat. "Zum Schluß geht man voll Schmerz
beiseit;/ Das macht die Unvorsichtigkeit" ("Finally they all walk off in
pain; / That is the result of carelessness") (1.279). This "carelessness"
is the "moment when one does not pay attention" in Vischer's
metaphysics of malicious objects.

Lower animals, especially insects, are merely an extension of the
malicious objects. They are all the more bothersome because they
have the added advantage of mobility and therefore can attack
humans more easily. Whether indoors or outdoors, there is no escape
from them. Flies and fleas prevent their tired victims from sleeping in
"Die Fliege" (The Fly) and "Die gestörte, aber glücklich wieder
errungene Nachtruhe" (Nocturnal Rest Disturbed but Happily Re-
gained). The summary execution of the attacker concludes each
picture story: the fly is squashed, and the flea burned in the flame of
the candle.

Vertebrates are depicted differently. In most of the early picture
stories, they, too, are cast in the role of man's adversary, but in many
cases their hostile acts are provoked initially by human aggression.
Only in his later works would Busch see animals as the ideal
representation of his interpretation of Schopenhauer's "will." In two
early strips, a calf and a pig display their natural stubbornness, but
their attempts at resistance are overcome. Their eventual fate makes

their struggle quite understandable: the calf is sold, presumably for slaughter. The last picture of "Der Bauer und sein Schwein" (The Peasant and His Pig) shows the poor animal lying on its back, its feet tied, the butcher kneeling next to it in the process of applying a big knife to its throat. Mercifully, the artist had his massive figure cover the animal's head so that we are spared the expression of agony on its face. The face of the peasant, however, who is holding the pig's tail, radiates extreme satisfaction: "Doch endlich schlachtet man das Schwein, / Da freute sich das Bäuerlein" ("But finally the pig is slaughtered, / Now our peasant was delighted") (1.203).

But frequently the animal triumphs over man, especially in cases where unprovoked attacks are ruthlessly avenged by the intended victim. The self-defense reaction is usually more effective than the original provocation. (This also holds for the stories dealing with acts of revenge among humans, another possible influence of the fairy tale.) When the elephant in "Die Rache des Elefanten" (The Elephant's Revenge) is wounded by an arrow, the luckless archer is dunked into water, almost fed to a crocodile, thoroughly hosed off, and finally deposited in a cactus. "Deceitful Heinrich" ("Der hinter-listige Heinrich") nearly succeeds in catching a gosling by luring it with a pretzel, but goose and gander come to the rescue. They lift the boy painfully by his ears and drop him through the chimney of his parents' home into his mother's oversized soup kettle. Three years earlier, Busch had already dealt with the theme of mischievous boys' attempts to abduct young birds, but in "Das Rabennest" (The Ravens' Nest) of 1861, it was the malicious object in the form of an overturning ladder that had protected the three young ravens. In "Der Affe und der Schusterjunge" (The Monkey and the Cobbler's Apprentice), the simian, whose tail is deliberately burned by a young man, becomes a furious avenger who tears out his attacker's hair, throws him to the ground, breaks a bottle over his head, and then turns on another person who comes to the youngster's defense. After he has stripped this fat gentleman of all the attributes of his dignity—top hat, elegant cane, hairpiece—the monkey goes to sleep, "voll Seelenruh' und Branntewein" ("filled with peace of mind and brandy") (1.273).

In these stories, the animal emerges as the central hero, with the human being serving as little more than a foil. Other early narratives deal almost exclusively with animals. The first of these, "Der Frosch und die beiden Enten" (The Frog and the Two Ducks), depicts the fight of the two birds for the possession of an unfortunate frog. During a very painful struggle the victim manages to escape, and the two

ducks in pursuit get stuck in a fence. Their fate is clear when a fat cook
grabs them, an oversized knife ominously held behind his back. A
year later, Busch returned to the theme of greed and jealousy in the
kingdom of the birds with "Der Kahnenkampf" (The Cockfight).
Here the two combatants are further individualized through proper
names; Gickerich and Gackerich fight over a pot of broth. The names
already indicate the almost perfect symmetry of the ensuing action:
one rooster seems the mirror image of the other. Again the unwillingness to share leads to mutual loss. Both animals fall into the broth,
the vessel overturns, and the dog Schnauzel can lick up the tasty
liquid while the two roosters walk off in defeat, dripping and deprived
of their most beautiful feathers.

Walter Huder points out that in this fable, similar to the plots of
other picture stories by Busch, "the misfortunes of Gickerich and
Gackerich, running amok, . . . are molds and archetypical models for
the cinematographic chases of Tom and Jerry."[6] Indeed, the patterns
established by Busch in his early animal stories are repeated
endlessly in today's animated cartoons and comic strips. Even the
violence of these cartoon fight scenes is very much in evidence in
Busch. The two ducks, trying to pull the poor frog apart, seem close to
their modern counterparts. But the "cruelty" of Busch's pictorial
narratives has to be seen in proper perspective. Folk tales served as
the first literary stimulus for the artist, and their exaggerated cruelty
is part of the nonrealistic atmosphere of the genre. Yet, he was quite
aware of the fact that the misfortune of others often tends to enhance
one's own feeling of well-being, and that proper distancing can even
transform this feeling into laughter. He discussed this question and
the role of his own technique:

Laughter is an expression of relative comfort. Frank, behind his stove, enjoys
the warmth even more when he sees Jack outside, blowing into his reddish
hands. But for public consumption, I have only used imaginary Jacks
["Phantasiehanseln"]. It is easier to set them up according to one's needs, and
to make them do and say what one wants . . . Such an outline being
["Konturwesen"] can easily free itself from the law of gravity and can,
especially if it is not beautiful, suffer a lot before we feel any pain. One looks at
the thing and hovers in comfortable self-awareness over the sufferings of the
world. (4.210)

This insight into the basic nature of laughter is as important as the
reference to *Konturwesen* that rarely invite identification on the part
of the viewer. When the animated cartoon adds motion to the line

drawing, we are less inclined to accept the rejection of Newton's laws, and in the case of three-dimensional representations, it becomes difficult not to identify with what is being depicted. While we can "hover over the sufferings of the world" as long as only "imaginary Jacks" do the suffering, our laughter dies away and a feeling of revulsion takes its place when we see real people in the same situation. This explains the failure of the many theatrical and cinematographic adaptations of Busch's picture stories. We can accept the fate of the bad boys of Corinth in verse and drawing as they become the victims of the big barrel they started to push: "Die bösen Buben von Korinth / Sind platt gewalzt, wie Kuchen sind" ("The bad boys of Corinth / Have been rolled flat like cakes") (1.163). In three-dimensional form, this image would be intolerable, as would be a realistic treatment of the painful stretching of the frog's legs.

With the designation of "The Cockfight" as a "fable," Huder touches on another important aspect of Busch's treatment of animals. As in the traditional fable—as well as in modern cartoons and comic strips—Gickerich and Gackerich and their like appear profoundly human. The last scene of "The Frog and the Two Ducks" shows this anthropomorphic aspect most clearly: the escaped victim of the greedy birds is recuperating, covered with a leaf as a blanket, dressed in a jacket, head bandaged, even smoking a long pipe: "Drei Wochen war der Frosch so krank! / Jetzt raucht er wieder, Gott sei Dank!" ("For three weeks the frog was so sick! / Now he is smoking again, thank goodness!") (1.109). Similarly, the final picture of "The Mouse" shows the rascal thumbing its nose at the two humans who were too clumsy to catch it and who instead transformed their bedroom into a scene of chaos. Such direct evidence of the human nature of the beast is not as frequent in later works, but most of Busch's animals are close to man in their facial expressions, and their motivation frequently resembles that of people who are liberated from social or cultural inhibitions.

Yet only a few of Busch's animal stories are true fables. In many cases it would be difficult to find a clear moral message. The "Cockfight" possibly comes closest to the traditional fable and could be illustrating the German proverb "Wenn zwei sich streiten, freut sich der Dritte" ("When two people are fighting, the third one benefits"). The fate of the two ducks seems to convey the same idea, with the cook being the lucky third party. But the author's sympathy is obviously on the side of the frog. It appears inconceivable that he wanted to demonstrate that the two rivals should have joined forces and shared the frog. The fable becomes ambiguous, and it might be better to enjoy it as the simple story about animals with human features, rather than attempting to read a moral into it.

That the difference between man and beast is a quantitative, not a qualitative one, seemed self-evident to the student of Darwin. Consequently, in his depiction of people, Busch frequently focused on stages of development or on circumstances where the superego is either not yet firmly enough established, or else is too weakened to inhibit actions. The ego shows itself as a destructive force, often bent on harming others even if there is no benefit to be derived. Alcohol sometimes brings out the real self. It is not by accident that the cobbler's apprentice carries a half-empty bottle of brandy in his hand when he makes the unprovoked attack on the monkey. Children, of course, do not need any liberation from social inhibitions not yet acquired. Accordingly, Busch's stories often feature variations on the theme of "bad boys" who act mischievously for no apparent external reason. Two boys, "young and cheerful," try to rob the ravens' nest. Deceitful Heinrich uses his mother's gift in order to snare the gosling. The rascals of Corinth enjoy teasing Diogenes in his barrel. This view of children was based on the author's own observation. In a long letter to his editor he once gave a vivid description of the petty acts of mischief wrought by his neighbor's son whom he watched through his window in fascination.[7] His experience agreed with what he later read in Schopenhauer's *Essays:* no animal is as cruel as man, and even a child of three or four will already act as the *"animal méchant par excellence."*[8]

Perhaps the most eloquent statement of Busch's anti-Rousseauistic position, to be reflected in so many of his works, can be found in a letter to Maria Anderson, who had sent him a pamphlet against hunting:

Your premise: "the unspoiled human being inherently experiences an unpleasant feeling whenever his fellow beings suffer" is wrong because it is *one-sided.* Suffering and torture rather exert a *frightful attraction,* causing horror and delight at the same time. —Have you ever noticed the expression of children watching a pig being slaughtered? . . . *Death, cruelty, lust*—here they are all together . . . When we are born, we are received by the good demon and by the evil demon who want to accompany us. The evil demon is usually the stronger and *healthier* one; it is the vital instinct. But the good demon *beckons to return,* and *good* children die early, their angel's wings have not been clipped off. —In short, the natural, unspoiled (?) human being, that is in particular the child, has to be predominantly evil, otherwise he cannot survive in this world. (B, 1.157)

With this view of children, which seems to combine the theory of the survival of the fittest with the concept of original sin, Busch was not only clearly opposing the Romantic belief in the natural innocence of children, but also the rationalistic creed that education could cure all ills. His tales have often been misinterpreted as only slightly more sophisticated equivalents of Heinrich Hoffmann's moralistic *Struwwelpeter* of 1848, an enormously successful book that attempted to teach children to behave like proper little adults. In the Frankfort physician's stories, all infractions of rules have horrible consequences. Busch's juvenile heroes have to pay dearly for their transgressions, too. But few of his tales come close to Hoffmann's didacticism. As early as 1860, "Der kleine Pepi mit der neuen Hose" (Little Pepi with His New Pants) shows that children do not learn from past experience or punishment. After having fallen into the water while wearing his new trousers (like Hoffmann's "Hans Guck-indieluft") and ruining them by sitting down in a container of pitch, Pepi is admonished by his father, whereupon he proceeds to steal some of his neighbor's syrup and falls into the big barrel, again damaging the just-repaired garment. "Trauriges Resultat einer vernachlässigten Erziehung" (Sad Result of a Neglected Education), an illustrated story in verse, is an obvious parody of the moralistic literature of the period. The very beginning sets the satirical tone:

> Ach, wie oft kommt uns zu Ohren,
> Daß ein Mensch was Böses tat,
> Was man sehr begreiflich findet,
> Wenn man etwas Bildung hat.

(Oh, how often we must hear / That someone did an evil deed / Which we find quite understandable / If we have a little education.) (1.75)

In mock indignation Busch complained about some parents who read the newspaper from morning to night, but fail to go to church even though they find time to go to the theater. As a result, they have only themselves to blame if they meet with a horrible end. Fritz is the unfortunate child of such negligent parents. He has the nasty habit of teasing the tailor Mr. Böckel, whose name is the Southern diminutive form of "Bock," "billy goat," by imitating the sound of bleating. The

enraged tailor decapitates him by means of his oversized scissors—a
motif that seems to come right out of *Struwwelpeter*. But the story
does not end there. The body is thrown into the water, eaten by a fish,
and finally discovered by the boy's mother when she cuts up the fish
in order to prepare dinner. In shock, she falls back and is pierced by
her giant kitchen knife. At this sight, the startled father, who has just
taken some snuff, sneezes so hard that he falls out of the window,
killing not only himself, but also Fritz's old aunt who happens to pass
by. A junk dealer is accused of the child's murder and is executed.
Eventually, however, justice catches up with the tailor who betrays
his guilty conscience when he hears the bleating of a goat. He is
sentenced to death, but takes his own life, using once again his big
scissors. Busch concludes with a warning:

> Ja, so geht es bösen Menschen.
> Schließlich kriegt man seinen Lohn.
> Darum, o ihr lieben Eltern,
> Gebt doch acht auf euern Sohn!

(Yes, that's what happens to bad people. / Eventually one gets his reward. /
Therefore, oh, dear parents, / Do look after your son!) (1.81)

It is hard to see how any reader could take this statement as a serious
piece of advice.

It is noteworthy that Fritz meets with a horrible end because he
teases a member of the adult establishment. This will become a
recurring theme in Busch's picture stories. The bad boys of Corinth
are killed as the result of their disturbing the peace of Diogenes. The
last picture shows the philosopher's barrel back in its original
position, with only the feet and the raised index finger of its
inhabitant visible: "Diogenes der Weise aber kroch ins Faß / Und
sprach: 'Ja, ja, das kommt von das !!' " ("But Diogenes, the wise man,
crawled into his barrel / And said: 'Yes, yes, that comes from that !!' ")
(1.163). The banality of this final statement, emphasized in the
original by the intentional use of incorrect grammar, makes the
"wisdom" of Diogenes appear rather questionable. He does not
display philosophical equanimity, but acts like a self-satisfied
bourgeois who is happy that law and order have been restored.
Rather than preaching a simplistic morality, Busch's ironic presentation questions societal values.

In his critical look at contemporary society, Busch sometimes comes close to Heine's irony. Both authors satirized the world of the bourgeois of which they themselves were a part. The deliberate destruction of a romantic mood that had been carefully established can be found in both writers. Busch's indebtedness to poems like Heine's "Wahrhaftig" (Truthfully) has been pointed out repeatedly. After presenting a string of popular "Romantic" words ("songs and stars and little flowers and eyes and moonlight and sunshine"), Heine immediately depreciates them by calling them "Zeug" ("stuff"). And in his "Gespräch auf der Paderborner Heide" (Conversation on the Heath of Paderborn), a sentimental atmosphere is created by what appears to be the sounds of distant violins and contrabasses, of hunters blowing their French horns in the forest and shepherds playing their shawms, of the singing of little angels as they are flapping their wings. But the sounds actually represent the squealing and grunting of pigs, the hogherd's whistle, the voices of the gooseboys, and the noise of their geese.[9] In "Adelens Spaziergang" (Adele's Walk), Busch's heroine takes a stroll through nature, and the vocabulary he employs—including a reference to the symbol of German Romanticism, the "blue flower" of Novalis—illustrates her perception of the world: "Sie pflückt auf frühlingsgrüner Au / Vergißmeinnicht, das Blümlein blau" ("She picks upon the spring-green mead / Forget-me-not, the little flower so blue") (1.280). This idealized image of nature collides with reality when a "green, wet, horribly large" frog jumps into the water. Adele properly faints, but an attack by ants brings her quickly back to her feet. Again an idyllic, pastoral mood seems indicated: "Ein Schäfer weidet in der Fern" ("A shepherd minds his flock afar"); but the very next line reveals new disillusionment, a new encounter with destructive reality: "Den Ziegenbock hat man nicht gern" ("The billy goat is not popular") (1.282).

The neo-Romantic glorification of the past and the idealization of history is gently mocked in "Eginhard und Emma" of 1864. A magnanimous Charlemagne moves everybody to tears by forgiving the eloping young couple; it is assumed that Emma and Eginhard will live happily ever after. But some skepticism seems warranted. Busch's earlier "Liebesgeschichten des Jeremias Pechvogel" (Jeremiah Luckless's Love Stories) related how the unfortunate protagonist was unable to find true love. The tone of those poems, and the technique of sudden changes in mood, are again reminiscent of Heine, who, after comparing his songs to little flowers and kisses for his beloved, indicates that he would rather see them as little peas so that he could cook a delicious soup for himself.[10] "Metaphern der Liebe" (Metaphors of Love) takes the flowery language of tender emotions literally and demonstrates in drawings and verse the fate of the unhappy lover who expects a lightning to flash from the glances of the object of his adoration that will crush him and break him up, and smash him into bone meal (see 1.98). And while Fernando, the lover in "Der Stern der Liebe" (The Star of Love), tells his beloved Elvira about the "beautiful, eternally shining star"—the "Star of Love"— Fernando, the husband, is too occupied with his beer stein to remember "what all those silly stars are called" (1.74–75).

Thus Busch's view of the institution of marriage is as critical as was his attitude toward education and the romanticization of nature and human emotions. Most of the marriages in the early picture stories are constant battles of the sexes. The peasant, returning home after his donkey has been killed by the malicious windmiller, is immediately set upon by his broom-wielding wife. In "Der hohle Zahn" (The Hollow Tooth), Friedrich Kracke tries to relieve his toothache by beating his wife. In the sequence of five pictures and brief captions, illustrating "Wie der Mann um den Hausschlüssel bitten lernt" (How the Husband Learns to Beg for the House Key), the spouses face each other in a power struggle that ends with the husband's humiliation. And yet, when Busch was asked in 1892, "How do you feel about marriage?" he responded: "I have a very high opinion of it if everything is completely honest." His definition of "love" was: "The longing to create unconsciously among two individuals a third entity that is perhaps better than oneself."[11]

In his autobiographical writings, Busch said very little about his graphic and literary style. When dealing with "imaginary Jacks" and "outline beings," he simply stated: "The trochee often seemed well suited for simple utterances; the line of the woodcut always practical for stylized amusing figures" (4.210). The "line of the woodcut" was decisive in shaping the style of his drawings. He would sometimes complain about the bothersome process of reproducing his sketches in the form of wood engravings, and it can also be asserted that some of the popularity of his picture stories was based on his xylographer's interpretation of public taste. But the forced reduction of complex patterns to simpler and more easily reproducible outlines proved beneficial for his artistic growth. His first contributions to Braun's periodicals, although indicative of his ability to capture characteristic forms and motions in bold lines, reflect the attempt to create three-dimensional illusions by employing halftones. Background details are frequently worked out almost to the point of interfering with the principal design. Gradually, the line emerges as the dominant element. Hatchings are used more selectively, and the attempt to give a realistic representation of light and shadow becomes rare. The trend toward more economical treatment of the objects depicted as well as of the facial and physical attributes of the characters is quite obvious.

In 1932 the cartoonist Thomas Theodor Heine, whose career had also started with drawings for *Fliegende Blätter* and who had become the leading pictorial commentator for the satirical journal *Simplicissimus*, wrote an appraisal of Busch as a graphic artist. He quoted the Impressionist Max Liebermann's view that drawing means leaving things out, but went on to say that a good drawing is more than the omission of the nonessential. The more an artist succeeds in reproducing life in a few lines, the closer is he to perfection: "A good drawing is always a new creation in simplified form, a kind of stenography of what was observed. Busch is the actual inventor of the shorthand of graphic representation. I do not know of any predecessor who succeeded, or who even attempted, to capture life in such concise lines, to conjure up through a simple stroke of the pen such incredibly intensified movement, such unforgettable characters along with the appropriate background, on a small sheet of paper."[12] This "shorthand of graphic representation" was mainly developed in the very active years from 1858 to 1864. By the time Busch created *Max und Moritz*, he had already arrived at what one critic called "the paradoxical combination of extreme realism and extreme abstraction."[13]

This period was equally important for the shaping of his literary style. While his sophistication and virtuosity in employing various techniques continued to grow, and while his "pure" poetry and his prose added certain new tones to his repertoire, the basic elements of his style are clear from his early poems and picture stories. In this respect, one can agree with Joseph Hofmiller's observation that the Munich *Bilderbogen* already reveal the total Wilhelm Busch.[14]

"Der kleine Pepi mit der neuen Hose" marks the last example of Busch's use of prose for a picture story. After 1861 (except for a few minor pieces authored in 1870–71), he employed verse exclusively, mainly in the form of rhymed couplets. His reference to the trochaic meter, quoted above, is rather curious. Most of his early verse is iambic; and even in his mature work, the trochee is by no means the preferred meter. The work for Braun provided Busch with an

opportunity to experiment until he arrived at the poetic form that
seemed most appropriate. Some early poems are indicative of this
experimentation. "Der Stern der Liebe" mixes verse and prose
passages very effectively. In "Der zu wachsame Hund" (Too Watch-
ful a Dog), the first line ends with the name of the dog's owner, Herr
Petermann. This name provides the single rhyme for the piece except
for a quatrain at the end spelling out the poem's moral. In "Jeremias
Pechvogel" of 1860, Busch used different rhyme schemes and meters
for each of the three parts of the poem. A closer look at the above tale
of unhappy love reveals a number of characteristic features. Busch's
technique of disillusionment is applied to the language. The first part
of the poem starts out—as frequently in Heine—like a traditional folk
song:

> Da draußen vor dem Tore,
> Da steht ein Lindenbaum,
> Wo ich so süß geträumet
> Der ersten Liebe Traum.

(Out there, before the gate, / There stands a linden tree, / Where I dreamed
so sweetly / The dream of my first love.) (1.42)

The vocabulary and the diction are unmistakably those of the folk
lyrics recorded during the Romantic period. Obviously, Wilhelm
Müller's "Der Lindenbaum" has served as a model. The beginning is
almost identical:

> Am Brunnen vor dem Tore
> Da steht ein Lindenbaum:
> Ich träumt in seinem Schatten
> So manchen süßen Traum.

(By the well, before the gate, / There stands a linden tree: / I dreamed in its
shadow / So many a sweet dream.)

The mood, established through the word choice, is broken when the
"beloved," to whom Jeremiah gave "a little ring of gold," is identified
as a "Nähmamsell," a seamstress. The Germanized form of the
French "mademoiselle" contributes to the alienation, and we are not
surprised when the ring shows up in the pawnbroker's window. In
the other two adventures of Jeremiah we find a similar mixture of
elements of folk poetry—including the use of impure rhyme—with
alienating foreign words. Both these stylistic idiosyncrasies can be

found in Heine as well. Sometimes the foreign terms are emphasized by carrying the rhyme, which adds a comic touch to what is said. Unlike Heine, Busch would frequently increase the linguistic alienation by spelling foreign words according to German rules of pronunciation. Other techniques that Busch was to use many times for comic effect help destroy the "Romantic" mood in this poem. His apparently carefree but actually very deliberate treatment of rhyme—such as the use of split rhyme—was combined in later poems with the use of enjambment (already in evidence here) to form some of his famous broken rhymes. Another humorous element is the combination of several words into a single monstrosity. Jeremiah's sweetheart writes her letters on "goldumsäumten Rosapostpapier" ("golden-edged pink-postal-paper"), and the lovely lady at the ball is "eau-de-Cologne-duftig" ("eau-de-Cologne-fragrant").

This tendency to play with the language remained one of the outstanding features of Busch's literary style. The incorporation of colloquialisms and even incorrect grammatical forms into his verse, often in juxtaposition with formal or antiquated expressions, first occurred during this period. In his early picture stories, he also began his manipulation of words in order to make them correspond to the desired rhyme pattern.

Busch's penchant for new words suggesting sounds or motions is also evident in these early picture stories. "Rumbums!" describes a falling chair (1.118), "Racksnacks!" the breaking of wood (1.129), "Schnurr!" a rapid fall through the chimney (1.236), "Schlapp!" the sudden opening of the lid of a box (1.237), and "Schwapp!" Heinrich's quick reach for the neck of the young goose (1.261). The author's inventiveness in this respect seems boundless, and the parallel with modern comic strips is obvious.

Another technique developed during these years is the humorous improper combination of unrelated entities or concepts. Since the names of the two women in "Müller und Schornsteinfeger" (Miller and Chimney Sweep), Nanni and Fanny, are nearly identical, Busch combines them into "Nann- und Fanny" (1.231). We have already encountered the monkey, sleeping "filled with peace of mind and brandy." When Heinrich falls into the broth, his mother pulls him out "mit einer Gabel und mit Müh' " ("with a fork and with effort") (1.264). Sigmund Freud quotes this phrase in his discussion of jokes and their relation to the unconscious without identifying Busch as the author, and then gives several quotations from Heine's works illustrating the same technique—thus again emphasizing the parallels between both writers.[15]

Related to this combinatory technique is the frequent occurrence of apparently isolated simple declarative statements in juxtaposition. But the connection can be established in the reader's mind or is given in the accompanying drawing. The story of the monkey's revenge starts with a description of the scene: "Der Affe sitzt in sanfter Ruh'—/ Der Schusterbube schleicht herzu" ("The monkey sits in gentle peace—/ The cobbler's apprentice sneaks along") (1.266). While the verb "sneak" may warn the reader as to the impending action, the picture—showing the youngster's face, the cigar in his mouth, the brandy under his arm—makes the suspicion almost a certainty. The ensuing events give the "gentle peace" of the first line a touch of irony. When the fat gentleman intervenes, the text reads: "Dem Herrn sein Hut ist noch ganz neu, / Dem Affen ist das einerlei" ("The gentleman his hat is still quite new, / That is of no concern to the monkey") (1.271). The picture illustrates this lack of concern: while the man is lying on the ground struggling to get up again, the monkey demolishes the hat by throwing the weight of his body on it. We saw the same technique at work in the encounter of Adele and the goat.

Sometimes the discrepancy between text and picture provides the comic element. When the two greedy ducks are described as "young and beautiful," the accompanying drawing renders that statement ironic (1.103). The story of the battle with the pesky fly ends with the very general sentiment: "Erquicklich ist die Mittagsruh, / Nur kommt man oftmals nicht dazu" ("An afternoon nap is invigorating, / But often one does not get to it") (1.120). The picture shows the slippered feet of the "Herr Inspektor" and next to them, on the floor, as if seen by a camera in close-up, the squashed remains of the annoying insect.

Some critics see "Naturgeschichtliches Alphabet" ("Alphabet of Natural History"), published by Braun in 1860, as an early demonstration of Busch's verbal and pictorial grotesque humor.[16] But Busch always insisted that he had not authored the couplets that accompany the drawings. Yet the little work must have appealed to him, since the technique of juxtaposing totally unrelated objects, held together, in this case, only by the same initial letter, was so similar to his own literary technique.

Munich was the city that had given Wilhelm Busch his start in art and literature, and the impact of the Bavarian surroundings is quite in evidence in his early work. Occasional use of local dialect, and names and cultural references connected with Southern Germany reflect the environment and were probably also of special appeal to his publisher's most immediate audience. Perhaps the technique of literary disillusionment was also influenced by a type of folk literature characteristic of Bavaria and the Alps. The *Marterl* is a memorial tablet, usually erected at the scene of a fatal accident. In a conversation, Busch referred to some of those epitaphs he had seen on his excursions from Munich, quoting the one he had liked best: "Wandrer, stehe still und weine—Hier ruhen meine Gebeine—Ich wollte, es wären Deine" ("Wanderer, stand still and weep—My mortal remains are resting here—I wish they were yours"). Busch added: "First he starts out in such a nice and friendly manner, but then the real rascal emerges."[17] This comment could serve as an adequate summary of the procedure frequently employed in his own work.

As Busch matured as an artist, the Bavarian local color gradually disappeared. By the time he was back in Wiedensahl, working on *Max und Moritz* and *Bilderpossen*, his North German background had reasserted itself. The years of trial and error, of searching for a personal mode of expression, were over; his artistic apprenticeship had ended.

II *The Village Humorist: The World of Wiedensahl (1864–1869)*

Busch once compared a weekly journal to a "voracious worm, with its fifty-two segments winding through the whole, long year" (B, 1.104). It is obvious that he remembered his work for Kaspar Braun's "voracious" publications and his concern that the constant pressure to produce might lead to a deterioration of his artistic work. So when Heinrich Richter in Dresden agreed to bring out *Bilderpossen*, the author's first book, it must have looked like an opportunity to achieve financial and artistic independence. The handsome little volume's failure to find a sizable audience was a double blow to the young writer.

In retrospect, it is not difficult to see why *Antics in Pictures* did not sell very well. Its four stories represent a strange mixture. The grotesque tale of "Ice Peter" was followed by an animal adventure, "Katze und Maus" ("Cat and Mouse"), and by "Krischan mit der Piepe" (Christian with the Pipe), Busch's only strip with the text entirely in Plattdeutsch. The concluding piece was a new version of "Hänsel und Gretel." The four stories might at first glance appear to be in the *Struwwelpeter* tradition, teaching children not to disobey their parents, not to smoke their father's tobacco, and not to be greedy. A closer look reveals greater complexity. The ending of "Ice Peter" probably was offensive to many, and the depiction of the parents' inane act of "preserving" their son's remains seems to mock their love for him. The harmless story of the cat chasing the mouse might be more easily accepted, but perhaps some adults did not want to expose their children to the picture of the cat's painful punishment. And, given the traditional attitude toward mice, the victory of the pesky little rodent offered a rather ambiguous moral lesson. It is not surprising that W. Harry Rogers, whose 1868 translation made the story accessible to a Victorian audience, felt compelled to add a clear "moral" to it.[18]

The intoxicating effect of tobacco on young Krischan is recorded by Busch in very imaginative drawings: as the child is smoking, the furniture in the room begins to dance around him, and while the pipe is growing longer—up to five times its original length—the smoke emerging from it takes the shape of weird and frightening specters. The skillful use of dialect shows Busch's mastery of language, but at the same time probably led to the loss of prospective South German readers. "Hänsel und Gretel" may have been inspired by Busch's involvement in the Munich artists' carnival of 1862 where an operatic treatment of this fairy tale, with his text and the music by Kremplsetzer, one of his Jung-München friends, had been performed. In his *Bilderpossen* version, the evil witch is assisted by her husband, a fat ogre who bears a striking resemblance to Kremplsetzer. After Hänsel and Gretel have disposed of the two, they return home where their mother is already waiting for them with the rod. Certainly the moral was quite clear in this case, but youthful readers, who had expected the traditional tearful reunion scene, must have been disappointed. Perhaps the rather free treatment of a story known almost by heart by many children caused some resentment. In addition, the pictures in the little book looked somewhat different from what the public had learned to associate with Busch from Braun's publications, since the format was new and Richter's wood engraver was not as familiar with this artist's style.

In view of the lack of success of *Bilderpossen*, it is understandable that Richter did not want to take a chance with the manuscript offered him free of charge by Busch in order to compensate him for his financial loss. Kaspar Braun had the foresight to buy all rights to that little "children's epic." He thus became the publisher of one of the most popular children's books of all times. The first edition of *Max und Moritz* came out in the summer of 1865. Others were to follow in rapid succession.

For this book Busch had abandoned the symmetric relationship between pictures and text characteristic of his earlier stories. Even though many drawings are accompanied by the customary rhymed couplets, there are also some pictures featuring only a single line—or no text at all. Longer verse passages are included, too, and the entire story is framed by a poetic foreword with only one illustration, and a conclusion that contains no pictorial adornment. Each of the seven pranks has a separate introduction. This is the general format Busch would use in most of the major picture stories to come.

The witty drawings and the humorous, easy-flowing verse of *Max und Moritz* found a ready audience, and the moral lesson seemed distinct: evil pranks, disrespect for one's elders, and the failure to become a conventional and productive member of society will lead to a bad end. For many generations, *Max und Moritz* represented an unsophisticated tale of crime and punishment in a rural setting. Only after two world wars had thoroughly disrupted bourgeois society and forced people to take a new look at traditional values, did careful readers begin to see that Busch's criticism was directed also— perhaps even primarily—at his society.

The foreword refers to Max and Moritz as misfits who refuse to listen to the advice of wise adults and, instead of mending their evil ways, ridicule those who want to mold them into better human beings. Significantly, the lines introducing the two boys specifically as "böse Kinder" ("bad children") are accompanied by a drawing of smiling youngsters, whose innocent faces reflect enjoyment of life, but hardly any inclination toward immorality (Ill. 2). But Busch's contemporaries failed to see the irony. They also did not understand the satire implied in the anticlimactic catalog of evil deeds that followed: instead of sitting still in church or school, the boys find it "more pleasant" and "more comfortable" to tease people, to torment animals, or to steal apples, pears, and plums (1.343).

This program is realized in the adventures that follow: Widow Bolte loses her three hens and her rooster. They are tricked into hanging themselves when they greedily swallow pieces of bread which the boys had tied together with string. The poor woman is even kept from enjoying the fried birds, as they are snatched from the pan and lifted through the chimney by means of a fishhook. Max and Moritz infuriate Böck, the tailor, by imitating the bleating of a goat.

In his blind rage he does not notice that the plank leading across the
brook in front of his house has been sawed into. Lämpel, the teacher,
loses his peace of mind and much of his hair in the explosion of his
favorite pipe, which had been filled with gunpowder. Uncle Fritz
discovers to his horror that someone put June bugs under his blanket,
and only after some violent struggle with the invaders can he go back
to sleep. The baker catches the pranksters when they try to steal
pretzels, but they escape again—not for long as it turns out. When
they cut holes into farmer Mecke's grain sacks, he bags them instead
of the wheat or rye he had intended to take to the mill. The miller
obligingly empties the sack into the grinding mechanism, and the
unfortunate youngsters are reduced to feed for geese.

Most of Busch's readers, who responded so favorably to the book,
would probably have agreed with the sentiment expressed by the
villagers who had been vexed by the two boys: "Als man dies im Dorf
erfuhr, / War von Trauer keine Spur" ("When this became known in
the village, / There was no trace of any sadness"). Everybody rejoices:
"Gott sei Dank! Nun ist's vorbei / Mit der Übeltäterei!!" ("Thank
heavens! The evildoings / Have ended now for good!!") (1.389). The
two exclamation marks, one for each of the executed criminals,
underscore the intensity of this unanimous opinion.

But what exactly happened to cause the ire of the good burghers?
"Mild and tender" Widow Bolte has lost the hens she had raised
specifically in order to enjoy their eggs and their meat and to use their
feathers in her quilt. These prosaic purposes, listed in the prologue to
the first chapter, provide a sobering backdrop to her emotional
reaction as she discovers the dead animals:

> "Fließet aus dem Aug', ihr Tränen!
> All mein Hoffen, all mein Sehnen,
> Meines Lebens schönster Traum
> Hängt an diesem Apfelbaum!!"

("Flow from my eyes, you tears! / All my hope, all my longing, / The most
beautiful dream of my life / Is hanging on this apple tree!!") (1.348)

And, "deeply grieved and filled with sorrow," she gets her knife to cut
the birds down before returning to her house "with a glance of silent
mourning" (1.349). The ironic discrepancy between the pomposity of
the pseudo-Romantic vocabulary expended here and the actual
happening should have given readers pause. The value system of

anybody for whom some fowl represented life's "most beautiful dream" appears questionable. Busch immediately reemphasized the shallowness of her sentiments by describing her thoughts in the first lines of the next chapter:

> Als die gute Witwe Bolte
> Sich von ihrem Schmerz erholte,
> Dachte sie so hin und her,
> Daß es wohl das beste wär',
> Die Verstorb'nen, die hinieden
> Schon so frühe abgeschieden,
> Ganz im stillen und in Ehren
> Gut gebraten zu verzehren.

(When good Widow Bolte had / Recovered from her grief, / She was pondering in her mind / That the best thing to do / For the deceased, who had / Passed away from this earth so early, / Would be, very quietly and with great respect, / To fry them nicely and to eat them.) (1.350)

The skill with which Busch leads up to this devastating (and unmasking) last line is reminiscent of the Bavarian epitaph he had admired.

The second victim is the tailor whose name is almost identical with that of his colleague in "Sad Result of a Neglected Education," and who is also overreacting to being teased about the similarity of his name with the word for billy goat.[19] This is the one thing that can make the gentle soul angry—otherwise he is willing to endure any abuse silently. Böck is a master of his trade, and Busch gives a long catalog of the various sewing operations he is carrying out, ending with this statement:

> Alles macht der Meister Böck,
> Denn das ist sein Lebenszweck.—
> —Drum so hat in der Gemeinde
> Jedermann ihn gern zum Freunde.

(All of this does Master Böck, / Because that is the purpose of his life.—/— Therefore everybody in the community / Enjoys having him for a friend.) (1. 355)

The values and priorities of a man who sees his life's aim in mending torn garments and replacing lost buttons seem lopsided. The word "therefore," connecting the two statements, is also revealing. The society portrayed here bases friendship on material considerations. Böck's popularity is the result of his usefulness to the community. His meekness is appreciated by the villagers, but his thinskinnedness when he is teased shows that his apparent gentleness is the result of severe repression.

The education of the youth of the community is in the hands of Mr. Lämpel. The name of this representative of bourgeois enlightenment is indicative: "Lämpel" means "small light." The kind of wisdom he dispenses becomes clear from his self-satisfied words immediately before his pipe blows up: " 'Ach!!'—spricht er—'die größte Freud' / Ist doch die Zufriedenheit!!!' " (" 'Ah!!'—says he—'the greatest joy / Is to be content!!!' ") (1. 365). The contrast between the triteness of this statement and the emphasis which is given to it—indicated by the triple exclamation mark—is striking. When he learns of the execution of his youthful tormentors his only comment is, "That is yet another example!"—echoing Böck's sentiment, "Malice is no aim of life!"

The introduction to the fifth chapter of *Max und Moritz* lists all the things that good nephews and nieces are expected to do in order to please uncles. This one-sided catalog of obligations, all designed to increase the relative's personal comfort, is the only reference to family life in the book. It holds little attraction for Max and Moritz. As in the previous cases, they have a keen eye for the particular weakness in their victim: the interruption of his night's rest turns Uncle Fritz into a wild man who "beats and tramples everything to death." Only after the floor is covered with June bug corpses does his peace of mind return. His reaction to the boys' death is: "Das kommt von dumme Witze!" ("That's the result of them silly jokes!")—a remark which in its deliberately incorrect grammar, in its banality, as well as in its complete lack of feeling, is reminiscent of Diogenes' comment on the death of the Max and Moritz of antiquity.

The penultimate chapter of the book starts with a general reference to "pious" bakers, and the sole representative of this group finds the two heroes covered with bread dough after they have fallen into his trough in their attempt to get at his pretzels. He treats them like two loaves of bread and shoves them into the oven. The glee in his face shows how much he enjoys his revenge, and his disappointment is obvious when they survive the ordeal and eat their way out of their shells of bread.

Max and Moritz meet their nemesis in the person of the farmer Mecke who is eagerly assisted by the miller. If we remember the earlier picture story about the peasant and the windmiller, and if we recall the face of the farmer while his obstinate pig was being slaughtered, we are already prepared for the lack of feeling exhibited by the two executioners. Except for the fact that Mecke speaks Plattdeutsch, his comment is identical with that of his earlier counterpart whose saw had cut his wife's nose: "Doch der brave Bauersmann / Dachte: 'Wat geiht meck dat an?!' " ("But the worthy peasant / Thought : 'What's that to me?!' ") (1. 389).

If we analyze the reactions of all the adults in this "children's epic," the same pattern of behavior emerges: each of these *petits bourgeois* reacts with the same vehemence and violence when his peace is disturbed. Neither the gentle tailor nor the good uncle and the wise teacher can accept such interference. Refusal to conform to the standards of society becomes a crime punishable by death. Creature comforts and material possessions assume supreme importance, so that the theft of fried chickens or pretzels, the destruction of a tobacco pipe and of a few grain sacks warrant execution. Of course there was "no trace of any sadness" when law and order had prevailed. *Max und Moritz* and *Struwwelpeter* are worlds apart, and the overwhelming success of Busch's picture story over several generations may be based on general misunderstanding or the readers' unwillingness to face the truth.

"Such an outline being . . . especially if it is not beautiful, [can] suffer a lot before we feel any pain." Indeed, neither the death of Widow Bolte's hens nor the explosion in Lämpel's study, nor even the terrible execution of the two boys causes us any pain. Busch's sophisticated balance between word and picture, and his tendency toward the grotesque effectively interfere with any emotional involvement. A comparison of the two roosters in the earlier "Cockfight" with the chickens in this story shows Busch's trend toward abstraction: his hens have been reduced to just enough characteristic lines to give us the desired association without creating the illusion of living animals. Thus their death hardly touches us, especially since they end their lives dangling side by side in perfect—and impossible—harmony from the apple tree. The accompanying text adds to the alienation by describing how "their necks grow long and longer" and their "chants become worried and more worried." Each one quickly lays one last egg before death arrives. The "worried chants" do not conjure up images of agony, and the fact that the rooster is included in the final production of eggs prevents any sympathetic reaction on the part of the reader (Ill. 3).

When Max and Moritz disappear into the mill hopper, we get one of Busch's frequent sound effects: "Rickeracke! Rickeracke! / Geht die Mühle mit Geknacke" (1. 388). Charles T. Brooks's translation comes close to this comic imitation of the noisy mechanism: "As the farmer turns his back, he / Hears the mill go 'creaky! cracky!' "[20] This is the end of the juvenile delinquents: "Hier kann man sie noch erblicken / Fein geschroten und in Stücken" ("Here one can still see them / Finely crushed and in pieces") (1. 388). The picture shows these "pieces" neatly arranged to form the clearly recognizable outlines of the two boys (Ill. 4). Yet, their metamorphosis is not complete: the geese greedily eat up the morsels, and the final drawing presents none of the humans who had appeared in the strip, but rather two very fat birds. The situation shown at the end of the Bolte chapters is ironically reversed: now the birds have eaten the boys. But one suspects that the pranksters will somehow reemerge.

Rudolph Dirks's *Katzenjammer Kids* (and the later *Captain and the Kids*) were patterned after Busch's picture story and first appeared in 1897 in Hearst's *New York Journal* as a challenge to Richard Outcault's "Yellow Kid" in Pulitzer's *New York World*. The very name of the strip betrays its Teutonic origin: "Katzenjammer," literally "cat's wailing," is a German slang term for "hangover," a condition Busch was to satirize frequently. The comic German accent used by Dirks in the dialogue contributed greatly to the success of his creation. But the first few installments were even closer to their model, since Dirks did not employ the speech balloons which he incorporated into later panels and which were to become a distinguishing feature of the comic strip. Thus Busch became one of the forerunners of this genre. His picture stories fill most of the classic requirements that define a comic strip: they are narratives with continuing casts of characters, told in pictures and text that are interdependent. Busch even pioneered the sound effects so common in modern comics. [21] Dirks's pranksters share with their models some physical traits and the inclination to play tricks on adults. But here the similarity ends. Busch's mastery in handling the language, his comic rhymes, the new words he created, his onomatopoetic skill, his inimitable graphic style, the ironic relationship between text and picture, the insightful criticism of bourgeois society are without equivalent in the American comic strips. And where Busch consciously restricted himself to the sphere he knew most intimately, the world of the village of Wiedensahl, Dirks and his successors were pursued by the "voracious worm with its fifty-two segments," and had

their Hans and Fritz travel to various exotic places in order to hold
their readers' interest.

Kaspar Braun's purchase of *Max und Moritz* had tied the author
once again to his publications, which continued to print Busch's
popular picture stories until 1871. Since Busch had relinquished all
rights to his successful book, only his publisher benefited financially
from the enthusiastic audience response. But the author's reputation
spread rapidly. In 1866 the first major collection of his picture stories
appeared in book form. The title of the volume, *Schnaken und
Schnurren* (Drolleries and Farces), underscored Busch's spiritual
return to Wiedensahl: "Schnaken" is a North German dialect term
that thus gained wide exposure in all German-speaking areas.

In some of the contributions for Braun, Busch returned to the
earlier format of pictures without text or with brief captions. The
best-known is "Ein Neujahrskonzert" ("A New Year's Concert") of
1865. This silent strip of fifteen brilliant drawings, featuring a pianist
and his listener, was republished later as "Der Virtuos" ("The
Virtuoso") and was to become second to *Max und Moritz* in popularity
during his lifetime. But in most cases Busch continued to augment
each drawing with a distich. His oeuvre during the years of his
association with his Munich publisher is impressive in sheer volume:
almost 190 separate contributions appeared in *Fliegende Blätter* and
Münchener Bilderbogen. While not all are masterpieces—Busch
referred to a small number of them as "Produkte des drängenden
Ernährungstriebes" ("products of the pressing food urge") (4. 151)—
the graphic and literary quality of the bulk of his work from this period
is high.

Two of the picture stories for the publisher Eduard Hallberger
deserve special mention. "Hans Huckebein, der Unglücksrabe"
(Hans Huckebein, Poor Devil or Hans Huckebein, the Unfortunate
Raven) came out in 1867. Huckebein is one of Busch's unforgettable
animal characters. He is individualized by his human name, and the
artist demonstrates great command of graphic means by giving the
bird facial features capable of expressing a wide range of emotions
without losing any genuine animal traits (Ill. 5).

Hans Huckebein is not a tame bird, and therefore he can represent
the "natural" drives and instincts that Busch also saw in children.
These drives are directed at destruction and power. This bird may be
an early demonstration of his interpretation of Schopenhauer's
concept of "will," seen as an absolute urge to live. Indeed, it is

probable that Busch had started his study of the works of the
pessimistic philosopher at the time when he first conceived of this
malevolent animal. But we should keep Theodor Heuss's warning in
mind that not everything in Busch's work ought to be blamed on
Schopenhauer.[22] We should also note the difference between the
aphoristic way of thinking displayed by the North German humorist
and the systematic approach taken by "der alte Brummbartel," "the
old grouch," as Busch once referred to the Frankfort philosopher (B,
1. 145).[23] Since Huckebein is a logical continuation of earlier characters, it is most likely that Busch found in Schopenhauer confirmation
of some of his own observations and did not make Schopenhauer's
philosophy a basis for his own creative work in any systematic fashion.

Huckebein asserts his superiority in his confrontations with human
beings. His sharp beak selects the finger and then the nose of the aunt
of his juvenile captor as targets. Indirectly, he causes bodily injury to
young Fritz as well: in the turbulence caused by his mischief, the aunt
accidentally pierces the boy's ear with a very pointed fork. Huckebein also emerges victorious in the joint onslaught of cat and dog who
fight with him for the possession of a bone. The end comes through
the malice of the inanimate object, facilitated, as so often in Busch's
work, by the effect of alcohol. After discovering a glass of liqueur, the
intoxicated bird becomes entangled in the aunt's knitting yarn and
hangs himself.

Busch referred to the animal's "black soul" and called Huckebein
"the greatest rogue" and "the evil one." The absolute use of this
terminology differs from the relativistic morality of the aunt, as expressed after the bird has bitten her finger: " 'Ach!'—ruft sie—'er ist
doch nicht gut!/Weil er mir was zuleide tut!!' " (" 'Ah!'—she cries—
'he is not good after all!/Because he is doing me harm!!' ") (1.480).
Good and evil are defined in terms of personal comforts or discom-
forts. Consequently, the aunt's final comments sound very much like
those of the villagers after Max and Moritz had died: " 'Die Bosheit
war sein Hauptpläsier, / Drum'—spricht die Tante—'hängt er hier!!' "
(" 'Wickedness was his principal pleasure, / Therefore'—says the
aunt—'he is hanging here!!' ") (1.498). The hypocrisy evident in the
facial expression and posture of her nephew as he listens to her
sermonizing shows the ineffectiveness of her moral doctrine.

Busch's insight into the problem of moral judgment was deeper.
He saw the tendency toward evil as inherited. In his view, much of

our behavior seems predetermined. Yet, that does not free us from the obligation to impose moral restrictions on ourselves. Even if it is fate that leads us into a predicament, we, not destiny, are responsible for our reaction. This is the message of a poem written in 1867 to clarify what he had tried to say in his picture story. The poem concludes with this reference to Huckebein's character: "Und lebte er auch noch einmal, / Er bliebe doch der alte Schlingel" ("And even if he lived again/ He would still remain the old rascal" (B, 2.300).

"Die kühne Müllerstochter" (The Fearless Daughter of the Miller) of 1868 is less complicated in its philosophical stance. It is the simple report about the killing of three evil robbers by a brave girl. One of the criminals is crushed by a millstone, the second dies when he becomes wrapped around the mill's gear shaft, and the third literally loses his head when he tries to inspect the money chest and the heroine closes the lid. But the careful understatement and the reification of human beings, with pictures that deliberately deviate from reality, create a grotesque atmosphere preventing the observer from taking the killings very seriously. Artistically, this strip is significant as Busch's first attempt to integrate text and picture into one typographical unit. But his lettering was not well suited for the process of wood engraving, and the overall esthetic impact was not up to the author's expectations (Ill. 6).

Busch's first contribution to the *Münchener Bilderbogen*—his first successful experiment with the genre of the picture story—had been a simple narrative, "Die kleinen Honigdiebe" (The Little Honey Thieves), showing how the bees avenged the theft of their product. Pastor Kleine's lessons in beekeeping had yielded a rather unexpected result. Busch's last substantial work to be published by Braun appeared exactly ten years later and was again devoted to bees and beekeeping: in 1869, the picture story *Schnurrdiburr oder die Bienen* (*Buzz Buzz, or The Bees*)[24] came out in book form. The author had retained his interest in the apiarian field and had even written articles for his uncle's *Bienenwirtschaftliches Centralblatt* (Journal of the Apicultural Association). His detailed background knowledge is obvious throughout the work, whether he deals with the roles of queen bee and drones, the problem of swarming, the attempts of the death's-head moth to penetrate the honeycomb, or with novel beekeeping techniques.

Schnurrdiburr is Busch's only unabashedly Romantic picture story, and perhaps for that reason never enjoyed the popularity

of some of his other works. His audience was used to cool and ironic depiction of bad boys and evil animals, not to warmth and sentiment and a happy ending for all instead of an execution.

In his introductory poem, Busch made quite clear that his gentle fairy tale did not aspire to lofty spheres: the Pegasus he mounts is a hobbyhorse, and the Muse he invokes in mock-classical fashion is asked to provide him with a pencil such as Faber in Nuremberg manufactures. The first chapter narrates in charming detail the activities inside beekeeper Dralle's hives on a beautiful spring morning. Dralle himself is introduced in the next chapter, but before we meet him, we take a look at his pig:

> Hans Dralle hat ein Schwein gar nett,
> Nur ist's nicht fett.

(Hans Dralle has a very nice pig, / But it's not fat) (2.11). The virtuosity with which the author uses the verse here in order to indicate the lacking weight is characteristic of the book. Similar irregularities or changes in verse form occur in appropriate places. When the text refers to Vergil, whose bees protected him against Roman legionnaires, it suddenly switches to classical meter, and then provides comic contrast by continuing with a very prosaic statement by Dralle in Plattdeutsch:

> Friedlich lächelt Virgil, umsäuselt von sumsenden Bienen;
> Aber die runzlichte Schar bärtiger Krieger entfleucht!
> "Wenn man de Schwarmeri nich wör!"
> Sagt Dralle—"Datt is dat Malör!"
>
> (2.32–33)

(In Wiemann's translation—which changes "Dralle" into "Tolen": " 'Vergil smileth serenely, fanned by his hivefuls of friendlies, / But the contingent of tough, crusty campaigners absconds.' "/ "Yes, but," says Tolen with a frown, / "This constant swarming gets me down.")[25]

But, before swarming, the bees attack Dralle's pig which becomes "nicely rounded" as a result and can be sold at a high price.

Besides Dralle, a few other major characters populate the picture story: Christine, Dralle's pretty daughter; Mr. Knörrje, the nice village teacher; Eugen, Knörrje's nephew, whose major goal is to get some of Dralle's honey. After various adventures that involve an unsuccessful attempt to recapture the escaped swarm of bees, encounters with a runaway dancing bear, an accidental swallowing of a frog (without any harm to animal or human), a moonlight rendez-vous of Christine and Knörrje, the apprehension of a thief who was after Dralle's beehives, all ends well. Knörrje and his beloved may get married, the bear is returned to the owner, the thief is taken away by the police, and even Eugen can enjoy some honey without punishment. The last chapter returns to the insect world and features the wedding celebration of the queen bee at the end of this eventful day. The final picture shows Busch's hobbyhorse, resting after all that hard work.

Schnurrdiburr marks the end of the first decade of Busch's work as a writer and graphic artist. He had returned to the world of Wiedensahl and Lüthorst. But the story of Hans Dralle and his bees remains the only attempt to depict this world as an idyll.

III   *Interlude: Religion and Politics (1870–1873)*

Ironically, the work to follow this gentle fairy tale was to lead to charges of blasphemy and pornography, culminating in a court case against Busch's new publisher, Moritz Schauenburg. When *Der heilige Antonius von Padua* (St. Anthony of Padua) appeared in May 1870, it elicited quick and strong reactions. Friend and foe alike interpreted the book as Busch's comment on the Vatican Council and the question of papal infallibility, and as his contribution to the increasingly bitter debate on the role of the Catholic church in Prussia. This confrontation, known as *Kulturkampf* (Culture Strug-gle), pitted Chancellor Bismarck against the Vatican. But Busch, despite his opposition to a political role for the church, had not intended to take a public stand in this controversy. In a letter of August 12, 1870, in which he supplied his publisher with material for the defense in the upcoming trial, he wrote:

I have never in my life occupied myself with tendentious matters. Whenever something struck me as funny I have tried to use it in my own way . . . That our little book is attracting so much unpleasant attention may be due in particular to the fact that it happened to come out at a time when the best judgment and thinking of a large segment of mankind is being attacked and condemned by Rome in the strongest way possible. Those who belong to that party in these matters may therefore easily assume that there is a deliberate tendency where only an accidental clash occurs, caused by the strong current from beyond the mountains. (B, 1.56–57)

The timing was indeed accidental. Busch had hoped for a much earlier date of publication. In December 1865, a first version of *Antonius* had been ready, but the original publisher had to drop the project; it took five years to find a successor. Parts of the work date back even further: the chapter dealing with St. Anthony's pilgrimage to Jerusalem is a revised version of a poem written in the 1850s (see 4.451–52). The penultimate chapter is an adaptation, with only minor changes, of "Die Versuchung des heiligen Antonius. Ein Ballett" (The Temptation of St. Anthony: A Ballet), probably completed in Munich in the fall of 1865 (2.529–36).

In his letter to Schauenburg, Busch tries to explain his position on religion and on the veneration of saints:

Having grown up within Protestant views, I was bound to find it strange that a true saint, a man without sin, could actually exist. The contrast between this widely held view and the concept of a real saint resulted in the more or less comic biographical sketch for which I utilized existing legends, and a specific name did not seem inappropriate for the representative of this category. The somewhat coarse tone found its support in legends, folk songs, and fairy tales that treat, for instance, St. Peter rather roughly without any embarrassment. The truly sacred, which all Christian religions share, has not been touched or violated anywhere. (B, 1.56–57)

Busch, who spent most of his life in Lutheran parsonages, was certainly influenced by the Protestant attitude toward sainthood. But his view was also a result of his occupation with Schopenhauer's philosophy. Busch did not believe in free will, as his interpretive poem about "Huckebein" indicates, and as he also makes clear in the introduction to the chapter dealing with St. Anthony's childhood: "So gilt doch dies Gesetz auf Erden:/ Wer mal so ist, muß auch so werden!" ("Nevertheless this law holds on earth:/ You must become what you happen to be!") (2.78). Nor could he accept the possibility of negating the will, as suggested by Schopenhauer. If Schopenhauer's position were taken to its logical conclusion, a single individual, through absolute asceticism, could bring the universe to a halt.[26]

In a letter to Maria Anderson, Busch called the philosopher's concept of sainthood a "whim" and continued: "If there had ever been a true saint, if anybody had ever been able to negate the will totally, the world would already be redeemed. Now the Jews continue to be right: The Messiah still has to arrive" (B, 1.145).

The preface to *Antonius* features a newspaper reader who, as Busch wrote his publisher, is upset by "the progress of the cultural movement that cannot be stopped, and who, for that reason, becomes somewhat comical" (B, 1.57). The news items listed deal with "malt extract and stock listings, machines for sewing and mowing and washing, foot-and-mouth disease and trichinosis," a catalog suggesting that Busch's reference to the "progress of the cultural movement" was not completely serious. The satiric intent becomes obvious when the newspaper reader reflects on the sorry state of church and religion. The use of broken rhyme makes his complaint particularly funny: "Wehe! Selbst im guten Öster-/Reiche tadelt man die Klöster" ("Alas! Even in good old Aus-/Tria convents and monasteries are being criticized") (2.77). The memory of St. Anthony is invoked because such a saint could serve as an example to our evil world.

Young Anthony, as he is described in the first chapter, is a hypocrite whose selfishness is hidden behind his image as a good Christian. When Busch listed the sources for the different chapters, he stated that this part was based on "ordinary observation." A motif from Boccaccio is used for the second chapter because "it seemed well suited for humorous pictorial representation." Anthony, as an adolescent, is chased into the sewers by a furious husband who finds him with his wife. Forswearing the pleasures of the world, the young man finds refuge in a monastery.

The material used for six of the following eight chapters was drawn from one source, which, again according to the above letter, led to the creation of the controversial picture story: "So Anthony came into being because I just happened to come across *The Blessed Virgin's Calendar*, dating back, I assume, to the beginning of the last century or the end of the previous one . . . You will find an abundance of the most peculiar things in said calendar, where a miracle of Mary's is told for each day of the year" (B, 1.56–57).[27] These miracles, attributed in this source to different saints, make up the *vita* of Busch's fictitious St. Anthony. It is noteworthy that he did not select the one legend from the life of St. Anthony to be found in the calendar, relating how the saint "made a donkey worship the Holy Sacrament and the Son of Mary in an open market square, thereby converting Bonivilla and many heretics."[28]

Busch's Anthony, as a young monk, becomes a skillful painter, and his portrait of Our Lady with the defeated devil at her feet wins him the approval of the Virgin and the hatred of Satan. The devil, appearing in the disguise of a young Carmelite nun, tempts him to flee from the monastery and to take along some of the order's treasures. Once outside, Satan triumphantly reveals himself and

Anthony is taken to prison. But Mary comes to the aid of her favorite painter, and the next morning finds the young monk before his easel and the devil in chains in the prison cell: "Recht nützlich ist die Malerei, / Wenn etwas Heiligkeit dabei" ("Painting is a rather useful craft / If a little holiness is connected with it") (2.95).

As Anthony matures, he totally accepts the Virgin as the guiding force in his life, and resisting temptation becomes easy for him. The special protection he enjoys becomes evident when she shields him in a violent storm, while a skeptical companion is killed by lightning. Mary also guards the monastery—and its wine cellar—in a devastating fire. When Bishop Rusticus decides to investigate Anthony's accomplishments, the monk hangs his hat on a sunbeam as a demonstration. As further proof of his ability to perform miracles, Anthony turns to a deaf-mute orphan boy and asks him for the names of his unknown parents. For the first time in his life, the boy begins to speak: "Bishop Rusticus, he is . . ." The bishop quickly stops him and acknowledges that Anthony is a true man of God. From this time on, St. Anthony is always seen with a halo (which has some practical uses, such as serving as a reading lamp at night, or providing a resting place for little birds). The incident related here was one of the "most peculiar things" Busch found in his source, where St. Goar demonstrated his powers to Bishop Rusticus by making a three-day-old orphan boy speak.

The *Calendar* also tells of the attempt by the immoral Caesaria to seduce St. Nerius while he hears her confession in her home. The saint asks the Blessed Virgin for support and runs down the stairs. According to Busch's source, the angry woman "throws a chair at him, which throw could have cost him his life; however, no harm came to him; but for thirty years after this victory, he did not have any carnal desires. It did not make any difference to him whether he touched or contemplated a woman or a rock."[29] Busch said that whenever something appeared funny to him, he attempted to use it in his own way, and it is easy to see this account as a stimulus. But he showed relative restraint: his Monika, "evil of mind, good of body," does not throw a chair. She simply marvels, as her attempt has failed, that none of the pious men she has met reacted that way.

It seems ironic that this chapter, along with the one showing the inability of the devil, in the guise of a beautiful ballet dancer, to seduce the aging saint, led to the charges of immorality or pornography. Busch's comments on those accusations are significant as a general statement: "Whoever meant to find even something *sensually titillating* in this little book, which is at best amusing, does not seem to realize that it is exactly the *parodistic treatment* of *form* and *situation* that must and shall directly militate against sensuality. What is meant to evoke laughter is not meant to seduce" (B, 1.57). Toward the end of the book, Busch's hero chooses a hermit's life in the woods. He vows not to move from the spot where he is sitting until there is a sign from heaven. Promptly, a wild pig appears and digs in the ground, a spring of fresh water opens up, and some truffles offer nourishment. From this time on, the pig becomes Anthony's permanent companion and also goes with him to the gates of heaven when the time has come for both. Despite the shouts of protest by Jews and Turks, the Virgin bids welcome to man and animal, saying that a worthy pig should not be excluded from where so many sheep are admitted. It was mainly on the basis of this scene that Schauenburg was charged with publishing blasphemous material. He was eventually acquitted, and the legal proceedings probably increased public interest in the book.

The lifting of the ban did not put an end to the criticism of *Der heilige Antonius von Padua*. The work is still controversial. A recent critic complained about the "revolting derision of Mary" in the story.[30] Another one called it a "crude satire" and bemoaned "Busch's pathological·hatred of Christian teachings and institutions, especially those of Catholicism."[31] Even some of the more moderate critics have occasionally regretted the fact that Busch selected this particular hero for his narrative. Not only is St. Anthony of Padua a very popular saint, but his biography is familiar to many people who therefore resent the complete lack of historical accuracy in Busch's portrayal. But—as the author stated—he did not intend to give an objective picture of one particular historic personage, but rather tried to depict a representative of a certain category. A specific name "did not seem inappropriate" for that purpose—just as more recently Max Frisch selected the name of "Andorra" for his fictitious country without implying any similarity with the Pyrenean state. But the choice of a different name might have blunted some of the attacks on Busch.[32] The deliberate anachronisms in the book—Anthony's cigar, Doctor Alopecius's umbrella, the devil in a tutu—underscore the ahistoric character of this biographical sketch.

Perhaps a factor contributing to the controversy was the somewhat diffused viewpoint in this picture story. Young Anthony is considerably less attractive than the "bad boys" Max and Moritz. The introductory passage makes it appear that he is predestined for

sainthood specifically through his negative characteristics. But
gradually, Busch seems to have developed a liking for his creation,
and there is no trace of hypocrisy in the older Anthony. The portrayal
of the hermit is charming and utterly without malice. Moritz Jahn
talks about the saint's attachment to his animal companion: "We
experience something here that we find very rarely in Busch's
writings: absolute goodness; in the last hours, as it were, of our
peculiar saint, a genuine moral quality becomes evident in him that
up to that point did not have a chance to develop: his capability for
grateful loyalty."[33] One reason for the late development of this trait in
Anthony may be the author's procedure of combining diverse legends
into the life story of one prototype.

Die fromme Helene (Pious Helena) was published by Bassermann
in May 1872. It was an immediate success. Two more editions
became necessary before the year ended. The seventeen chapters of
Helena's biography amount to a deliberate parody of an *Entwicklungsroman*, a novel describing the development of an individual.
We observe the heroine's childhood, spent with her aging uncle
and aunt. Then she tries a middle-class existence by herself until
she realizes that her youth will soon be gone. Her marriage of
convenience with "Schmöck & Co." results in frustration that leads to
an adulterous affair with her childhood sweetheart, Cousin Frank,
who has grown up to become a priest. The accidental death of
Helena's husband is followed by the equally unexpected murder of
her lover by the butler in a fit of jealousy over the favors of a kitchen
maid. In the final stage of her life, alcohol competes with religion as a
means of moral support, and her drinking brings about a fiery death.

In terms of inner development, Helena goes from mischievous
child to young woman with a zest for life, to youngish spinster who
vents her frustration on an unfortunate cat, to sexually and emotion-
ally dissatisfied young wife and wealthy matron. Her active interest in
religion is hypocritical, and her eventual renunciation of all worldly
life is not based on any spiritual experience, but rather on the
realization that there is nobody left to care for her.

A significant segment of the *Kulturkampf* audience saw this book as
Busch's second attack on the Catholic church and connected *Die
fromme Helene* immediately with *Der heilige Antonius*. But, except
for some similarity in the treatment of certain religious motifs, the
two works have little in common. The setting is now contemporary,
not medieval. Helena is depicted as a big-city girl, and the references
to nineteenth century Frankfort are quite prominent. She is not a

composite character like Anthony, even though some aspects of her development are not treated in detail.

Helena's youthful pranks appear as a natural reaction to the shallow preachments of the adult generation and correspond to behavior patterns that Busch had observed in children. The warnings she receives from her relatives make morality a function of age and physical capability. Her uncle admonishes her "as a human being and as a Christian" to refrain from evil, which is pleasant while we are doing it but annoying afterwards. Her aunt adds that the wise maxims of old people should be followed: "Die haben alles hinter sich / Und sind, gottlob! recht tugendlich!" ("They have everything behind them / And are, thank goodness! quite virtuous!") (2.206). Of course this advice is totally ineffective, and Helena immediately proceeds to sew up the sleeves and the collar of her uncle's nightshirt, thereby creating havoc when he goes to bed. A few years later, she is sent away after having once again invaded the comfort of her relatives' bedroom, this time by pulling away their blanket by means of a fishline. Putting a frog into Uncle Nolte's snuffbox is not her idea, but she shares the joy over Cousin Frank's successful prank.

Helena's adolescent curiosity as she watches Frank through the keyhole, her flirtations with him, and the love letter she composes after his departure, all reflect the natural behavior of a teenage woman. Friedrich Bohne suggests that the breaking of her statue of the Medicean Venus by an excited cat marks a significant turning point. The shattered sculpture seems to assume Helena's facial features, indicating that the heroine has reached the age when the power of the love goddess begins to wane.[34] The next chapter is devoted to an extensive description of Helena's cosmetic manipulations in an effort to remain attractive. It culminates in her decision to get married immediately. When her husband shows more interest in culinary delights than in the pleasures she offers him, religion becomes her emotional outlet. The stage of having "everything behind" her and being "thank goodness! quite virtuous"—at least as far as her image is concerned—has been reached prematurely. Perhaps the important difference between Helena and Anthony is that in his case religion becomes a genuine way of life after he has started out as a hypocritical little boy, whereas her natural impulses have become stunted and repressed, and she grows into a religious hypocrite. Consequently, Anthony and his pig may enter heaven, but her soul cannot be saved. That Frank is already waiting for her in hell's cauldron seems logical since his development took a course

parallel to hers. He is condemned—not because he is a Roman
Catholic priest, but because he is a sanctimonious Pharisee. But
during the *Kulturkampf* era, many readers failed to see that distinction.

By selecting contemporary Frankfort as the scene, Busch was able
to utilize some of his observations from the years of his friendship
with the Kessler family (whose villa appears to have been used as the
model for the Schmöck home). He now had the opportunity to voice
some social and cultural criticism that had no place in the previous
picture story.

The viewpoint of the disgusted observer whose remarks make up
the first chapter seems close to that of the newspaper reader in the
introduction to *Antonius*. He laments the immoral press that pub-
licizes various sinful excesses, including the Jacques Offenbach
productions in the Thalia Theater. *La Belle Hélène* was actually
staged in Frankfort during the period of Busch's acquaintance with
the Kesslers. Balls, concerts, and Sunday promenades give vain
people a chance to display the latest fashions. There are the evil
circles of beer hall politicians who mouth liberal slogans and even
express their hatred of the Holy Father. And there is the Jew who
wriggles his way to the stock exchange, his feet as crooked as his nose
and pants, "deeply corrupted and without a soul" (2. 204). The
context should make it clear that we have here the caricature of the
Jewish stereotype as seen by the nineteenth-century bourgeois. This
exaggerated description reflects the same biased view as the rantings
about evil liberal politicians and the goings-on in concert halls and
theaters. Yet this passage continues to be interpreted as an expression of Busch's alleged anti-Semitism.[35]

It is from the corrupting influence of this metropolis that young
Helena is to be protected. She is taken to the country, where gentle
sheep and pious lambs can be found, where virtue and reason prevail,
and where her relatives reside. The equation between "gentle sheep"
and "pious lambs" on one hand and Helena's relatives on the other is
clear. As in *Max und Moritz*, the reaction of the adults to any
disturbance of their orderly world strips off the veneer of gentleness,
"virtue," and "reason." A tug on the blanket turns the Noltes, who
had been sleeping peacefully and hand in hand, into bitter enemies.
It is noteworthy that Helena, as an adult, displays the same sudden
release of suppressed emotions when she very deliberately sets fire to
the tail of the cat responsible for the breakage in her apartment.

The four final drawings of the story show Uncle Nolte's reaction to the death of his niece. We are reminded of the conclusions of "Hans Huckebein" and *Max und Moritz* when Nolte states that he had predicted such outcome from the beginning, and when he finishes by saying with great satisfaction: "Ei ja!—da bin ich wirklich froh!/ Denn, Gott sei Dank! Ich bin nicht so!!" ("Ah yes!—I am really glad!/ Because, thank goodness! I am not like that!!") (2. 293). Immediately preceding this pharisaic exclamation, we find another statement that has become one of the best-known quotations from Busch's work: "Das Gute—dieser Satz steht fest—/ Ist stets das Böse, was man läßt!" ("The Good—and this is always true—/ Is just the evil we don't do!") (2. 293). The context suggests that this is yet another of Uncle Nolte's banalities, pronounced with great seriousness and with raised forefinger for emphasis. The reader is asked to accept a definition of ethical values as being "always true," even though it seems to reflect only the limited vision of a *petit bourgeois* evidently incapable of grasping the concept of "good" per se.[36] But Busch himself singled out this particular phrase as one resulting from a great deal of thinking and of hard work. Certainly he was not only referring to the poetic mechanism involved. We could interpret this statement, in terms of ethical pessimism based on Schopenhauer, as follows: we have the tendency to be as we are, that is, to affirm our will which is directed at harming others. Voluntary renunciation of that will would be truly "good." Young Helena, who says after each prank, "I won't ever do it again!" is as incapable of going against her nature as was Hans Huckebein. Did Busch really intend to make narrow-minded Uncle Nolte a spokesman for Schopenhauer's philosophy? Any one-sided interpretation would overlook the ambiguity that is so characteristic of much of Busch's work.

In 1870, Busch could state that he had never occupied himself with "tendentious matters." Later, however, he had to mention "one allegorical tendentious piece" as the significant exception to the rule that he created his works mainly for his own pleasure (4.151). This book was *Pater Filucius* (Father Filucius), published in November 1872. This third of his *Kulturkampf* picture stories is the only major work he created in direct response to a suggestion by another person. Apparently buoyed by the acquittal in the *Antonius* case and by the enthusiastic response to that book and to *Helene,* and hoping to benefit from the political climate, Busch's new publisher wrote to his friend: "I know that one may not make any suggestions to you; however, the Pope, supporters of infallibility, Jesuits, and bigoted pietists are the targets everybody turns to now, and arrows shot at those targets will be applauded."[37] The time seemed indeed appropriate. Bismarck's attempts to curtail the role of the Catholic church in the newly established German Reich were welcomed by many, and legislation outlawing the Jesuit order was seen as imminent. Busch strongly approved of Bismarck's efforts to unite the German-speaking people. Quite uncharacteristically, he went along with Bassermann's idea and requested reference material on Jesuitism, but was rather appalled by the tone of one of the sources. Within a few weeks, he had completed his new picture story.

Father Filucius, the evil Jesuit, tries to pervert the household of young Gottlieb Michael, who lives with his aunts Petrine and Pauline, and who is in love with the pretty niece Angelika. When the girl energetically repulses the priest's amorous advances, he turns to Aunt Petrine. He establishes a close friendship with her and presents her with Schrupp, an ugly little dog. Schrupp's fleas bother everybody except her until Gottlieb manages to cleanse the animal. But the dog continues to do damage and has to be punished. When Gottlieb surprises Filucius in a romantic situation with Petrine and forcefully removes him from the house, the Jesuit swears revenge. His attempt to poison Gottlieb fails, and he solicits the help of two criminals, Inter-Nazi and Jean Lecaq, in order to kill his enemy. Angelika overhears their plotting, and Gottlieb asks his friends for support. Hiebel, the watchman, Fibel, the teacher, and Bullerstiebel, the farmer, are happy to help, and jointly they overcome the three intruders, beat them severely, and throw them—and Schrupp—out. The happy conclusion is the announcement of Gottlieb's upcoming marriage with Angelika.

Pater Filucius was conceived as an allegorical satire. The name of the priest, the Latinized form of the French *filou* ("crook"), indicates the slant. In a letter to Bassermann, Busch interpreted the story as follows:

I am glad that you like the Fil. that came into being as a result of your suggestion, after all. If you look at it as a family affair, it could be called extreme, if you take it politically, it is not, I think; it simply expresses the most recent wishes of the state which cannot quite coincide with the wishes of the Church, to be sure. German Michael with the Protestant and Catholic housekeeping aunts and the niece, the State Church; the Jesuit with deception, poison and dagger, in alliance with other enemy forces; the ultramontane press plus appendage, introduced by him—these things provide the allegorical background on which the little family piece is based. I assume that you noticed, too, the military, agricultural, and teaching professions. (B, 1.81–82)

Later he further clarified the "other enemy forces," Inter-Nazi and Jean Lecaq, as referring to the (international) Social Democrats and the French (B, 1.95).

The introductory passage to his letter, and the need Busch felt to provide a key for his allegory, indicate his uneasiness, and he soon referred to the book as an "allegorical ephemerid" (B, 1.92). He had strayed into a field that was alien to him, and the work shows it. Busch was successful as a social commentator and critic, but he was not suited to be the mouthpiece for "the most recent wishes of the state." The satire is heavy. Filucius is presented as so evil and so lacking in any human traits that he elicits little emotional response from the reader. Despite some elements of verbal and graphic grotesque, the work is devoid of humor. The public echo says more about the political climate of the day than about the quality of the book. "Imaginary Jacks" and political caricature are mutually exclusive.

The other product of the busy year 1872, *Bilder zur Jobsiade* (Pictures for the Jobsiad), is also uncharacteristic of Busch's work. It represents the attempt to illustrate the work of another author, Carl Arnold Kortum's humorous epic of 1784, *Leben, Meynungen und Thaten von Hieronimus Jobs dem Kandidaten* (Life, Opinions, and Deeds of Hieronymus Jobs the Candidate). Busch obviously enjoyed the mock-heroic biography of Hieronymus who, after his wild student days, an unsuccessful effort to become a minister, a short career as village teacher, and an abortive stage debut, becomes the town's night watchman. Far from merely providing illustrations for Kortum's text, Busch also revised the poem itself, shortening it drastically in places and adding his own verses in others. Kortum is largely responsible for the humorous chapter dealing with Job's theological examination. Another chapter, added by Busch, shows the Candidate's guest sermon in his hometown church. The platitudes of the sermon, which was written for Jobs by a fellow student, are accompanied by wildly theatrical gestures. The comic effect produced attests to Busch's unique ability to blend word and picture. It is significant that this time his target was Protestant rather than Catholic clergy.

Busch's appreciation of Bismarck's accomplishments did not amount to blind admiration, and later, when invited to visit the

Chancellor, he refused. The creation of the criminal Inter-Nazi (and his absurd pact with the Jesuit) has to be contrasted with the fact that Busch was an avid reader of Social Democratic newspapers and sympathized with many of the goals of the labor movement. All his life he remained too critical an observer ever to embrace completely any political ideology.[38] So we find little in his work that is blatantly political. Besides *Filucius,* there are only a few shorter pieces directly relating to the Franco-Prussian War, contributions that were clearly "products of the pressing food urge." His major picture story of 1873 shows how much of a passing phenomenon the political engagement had been for Busch.

Der Gerburtstag oder die Partikularisten (The Birthday or The Particularists) is set in the fictitious village of Milbenau in North Germany. The villagers decide to express their loyalty to their former king, who had been deposed by the Prussians, by sending him a birthday gift. Plans are discussed in Mother Köhm's tavern, "The White Horse." The fat mayor is worried about the rebellious attitudes displayed, even though he is secretly anti-Prussian as well. The suggestion of Pille, the pharmacist, to present their beloved monarch with a case of his special elixir is enthusiastically accepted. But the man who is to carry the load to the coach station decides to try a bottle himself, becomes intoxicated, and drops the entire burden into the village pond. As a result, the geese, the pigs, and the goat become exceedingly happy after drinking from the water, and eventually turn against the people. The attack is led by the billy goat, whose target is Böck, the tailor. The mayor is carried off by a pig; Pille, all dressed up for the trip to the city, is thrown into the mud. The only one to benefit is Mother Köhm because everybody needs a drink after that experience.

A new decision is reached: a delegation will take a large basket of eggs to the king. But the carriage overturns. Tall Korte, the veteran in his old dress uniform, and the two maids of honor offer a pitiful sight, covered, as they are, with broken eggs. A penetrating smell indicates that not all donations were fresh, and sly Krischan Stinkel tells his wife how he had tried to get rid of some of their rotten eggs. At Mother Köhm's, another proposal is adopted: everybody will contribute some butter, and Knickebieter, the baker, will shape it into a giant sculpture of a hen. The baker goes to work and soon discovers that one of the balls of butter is filled with mashed potatoes—most certainly Krischan Stinkel's gift. A big hen emerges under his skillful hands, and the excess butter is put aside in a keg for his own use. The sculpture seems too large for his taste, so a new bird is formed, much smaller in size, while his keg fills up with "excess" butter. The dimensions of the gift are a disappointment for the villagers, but they voice their approval. Another accident prevents the delivery of the present: the cart horse, stung by a horsefly, moves suddenly, and the mayor is thrown on top of the work of art, thereby destroying it. Now it is too late to make other arrangements, and everybody retires to the "White Horse" tavern. An attempt to place the blame for the various failures leads to a brawl, but eventually peace is restored, and everybody has another drink. The last picture shows Mother Köhm's happy face. Upon Bassermann's insistence, Busch finally agreed to strike the concluding couplet: "Ja, selig ist der fromme Christ, / Wenn er nur gut bei Kasse ist!" ("Yes, a good Christian is delighted / If he is only well off for cash!") (2.550).

Obviously Busch enjoyed his portrayal of rural society. The inhabitants of Milbenau are three-dimensional human beings, not allegorical representations. Their weaknesses are shown with understanding and humor. The only person whose image is somewhat negative is the opportunistic mayor. Busch's use of dialogue is very effective. By having some people speak Plattdeutsch and others High German in various degrees of grammatical correctness, he skillfully sketched the social and educational structure of the community. The political background is de-emphasized. The citizens of Milbenau want to honor a king who has been deposed as a result of the establishment of the new German Reich. But the events in the village could as well be completely unrelated to any political demonstration. Some references to politics are so subtle as to be missed by most readers. The Guelphic party, the North German loyalists hoping for the return of the kings of Hanover, had selected the white horse as their symbol, and the name of Mother Köhm's tavern thus assumes a special meaning. When the carriage overturns, Korte and the two girls emerge all "white and yellow." Those were the traditional colors of Hanover.

Bassermann would have preferred another *Filucius*. He suggested a different ending, glorifying Prussia and the German Reich. Busch's response was unequivocal: "Your proposition would amount to a transformation and, in addition, give the story a certain character that I have carefully avoided. Humor above all, and little else beyond that!" (B, 1.103). His brief and not very happy excursion into the field of political art was over.

CHAPTER 3

The Bourgeoisie Satirized: Busch's Later Picture Stories

I Of Average People: The World of the Bourgeois (1874–1879)

THE collection of shorter picture stories and poems, with and
without illustrations, published a year after *The Birthday* provides a link between Busch's earliest literary attempts and his first
book of serious poetry. Some of the pieces in *Dideldum* (Tralira)
seem to recall the hours spent in Munich taverns and coffeehouses.
"Trinklied" (Drinking Song), which has some *Kulturkampf* over-
tones, is illustrated with eight humorous self-portraits. A number
of the picture stories could easily have been included in Braun's
publications: a puff of wind takes away elegant Joseph's top hat and
prevents him from going to church; a frustrated gardener tries to
kill an annoying mole; young Hermine attends a dance against her
parents' will and meets with misfortune when trying to sneak back
into the house.

Not everything in *Dideldum* follows earlier models, however.
There is a new poetic tone that should have prepared the attentive
reader for Busch's impending turn toward philosophical poetry. In
"Summa Summarum," the forty-one-year-old author paused to
"clean his glasses" and to go through the account book of his life to
see how he had utilized his time. The final realization is: "Denn
die Summe unseres Lebens / Sind die Stunden, wo wir lieben"
("For the sum total of one's life / Are the hours spent in love")
(2.489). Perhaps his relationship with Johanna Kessler had contributed to this insight. Perhaps Wilhelm Busch, the bachelor, found
himself in the same reflective mood as displayed by bachelor
Tobias Knopp at the beginning of his next picture story.

Abenteuer eines Junggesellen (A Bachelor's Adventures) appeared
in November 1875, and before the year ended, ten thousand

copies had been sold. Busch had conceived of this book as being complete in itself, concluding with the hero's wedding. The last picture, showing a little cupid tactfully closing the bed curtains, and the accompanying couplet were meant to indicate finality: "Na, nun hat er sein Ruh. / Ratsch!—Man zieht den Vorhang zu" ("Well, now he has his peace. / Rip!—The curtain is being drawn") (3.82). But the curtain had to be opened and closed two more times: *Herr und Frau Knopp* was published in 1876, and *Julchen* (Little Julie) of 1877 completed the trilogy. The final vignette of *A Bachelor's Adventures* did symbolize the end of a significant period in Busch's graphic art, however: the sketch of the amoretto was the last of his drawings that had to be reproduced on wood. From then on, a photomechanical process made it possible to prepare plates from the original drawings (Ill. 7).

Tobias Knopp's biography starts at a point when the roly-poly bachelor is plagued by a strong feeling of dissatisfaction. His life has been orderly and comfortable—his trusty housekeeper Dorothy takes care of "boots, bed, coffee," and is always willing to reattach missing buttons—but he is sensing the lack of something. He is suddenly aware of the fact that his youth is over. His hair is gone, and even several weeks spent in a health spa fail to reduce his waistline permanently. He muses about the many things in this world that are unpleasant: "Roses, aunts, female cousins, and carnations" are destined to wilt, and he himself will eventually be "crossed out with a thick line" (3.13). The equation of female relatives and flowers might be interpreted as a philosophical insight into the essential sameness of all organic beings, but it more likely reflects the narrow and materialistic view of an egocentric who classifies all phenomena according to what is or is not pleasant for him. Tobias bemoans the fact that the eye that will read one day that "Knopp was there and has gone" will shed no tear; nobody will be "bothered" or "have inconveniences" when he is buried (3.13). These melancholy thoughts are a remarkable translation of man's eternal desire for immortality and for lasting deeds into a philistine nightmare of a meaningless note in the obituary column and of an unadorned grave. This leads to his decision to find a wife. It is only logical that, once that goal is reached and a child has been fathered and brought up to be married, there is no further function left. So the last drawings of the trilogy show a shriveled Tobias Knopp: "Knopp der hat hinieden nun / Eigentlich nichts mehr zu tun.—/ Er hat seinen Zweck erfüllt" ("Now Knopp has on this earth / Actually nothing left to do.—/ He has accomplished his purpose") (3.204).

Knopp's adventures in his search for a spouse severely test his determination to get married. Adele, the love of his youth, has lost all her physical charms, and her possessive attitude toward him is a frightening experience. The insights he gains into marital problems and family life, as he continues to visit old friends, are depressing. Knarrtje, the forester, is a cuckold. Cheerful Babbelmann has turned into a sanctimonious hypocrite under the influence of his wife. Mücke's marriage seems ideal at first, until it becomes evident that he deceives his wife with a pretty waitress. But the most grotesque situation awaits Knopp when he finds his friend Sauerbrot in a jubilant mood: his wife has died and lies in her coffin in the next room. He is free again. All those foolish expenses for her whims are behind him. But his happiness is of short duration: "Knarr!—da öffnet sich die Tür.) Wehe! Wer tritt da herfür!?/ Madam Sauerbrot, die schein-/ Tot gewesen, tritt herein" ("Creak!—the door is opening. / Woe! Who is emerging there!?/ Madame Sauerbrot, who only seem-/ Ingly was dead, is entering") (3.66). The shock kills him instantly. The broken rhyme explaining Mrs. Sauerbrot's death as only apparent, and the grotesque drawing illustrating the friend's paralysis by transforming the outlines of his figure into a few rigid lines, produce an alienating and comic effect (Ill. 8).

If the traveling bachelor had thought of perpetuating his earthly existence by becoming a father, the family scenes he witnessed should have given him pause. The home of Plünne, the sexton, is dominated by his three children, who are engaged in various malicious or unattractive activities. Two other episodes gave Busch the opportunity to present more examples of the inherent badness in children, and at the same time to satirize extremes in educational philosophy. Rector Debisch punishes his son Kuno by looking at him sternly, and by telling him to be ashamed and to leave the room:

> Das ist Debisch sein Prinzip:
> Oberflächlich ist der Hieb.
> Nur des Geistes Kraft allein
> Schneidet in die Seele ein.

(That is Debisch's principle:/ A thrashing is just on the surface./ Only the power of the mind / Can make a deep impression on the soul.) (3.29)

The smirk on Kuno's face attests to the total ineffectiveness of "Debisch's principle." But the opposite approach, as demonstrated by Master Druff, proves equally incapable of "making a deep impression on the soul":

> Druff hat aber diese Regel:
> Prügel machen frisch und kregel
> Und erweisen sich probat
> Ganz besonders vor der Tat.

(But Druff has this rule:/ A caning keeps a child fresh and lively / And is very effective / Particularly before the act.) (3.30)

So Franz is flogged in order to assure his good behavior at the rural ball he is allowed to attend with his parents and their visitor. He promptly makes Knopp the embarrassed victim of his pranks.

A budding romance with the daughter of his friend Piepo ends suddenly when Tobias finds himself in a disconcerting situation as the result of falling asleep in the bathroom. His encounter with Krökel, the hermit, reassures him in his decision to find a wife, but also convinces him that there is no need to roam so far afield. The unkempt recluse had declared that his one and only love was Saint Emmerentia. His withdrawal from civilization and renunciation of all worldly things is not too convincing: he immediately appropriates Knopp's liquor bottle and drinks himself into a stupor. On the basis of this experience, Knopp decides that "love per distance" is not for him. He concludes his odyssey where it began. His "nice, good Dorothy" is just making the bed when he returns and asks his question: " 'Mädchen,'—spricht er—'sag mir ob—'/ Und sie lächelt: 'Ja, Herr Knopp!' " (" 'Girl,'—he says—'tell me whether—'/ And she smiles: 'Yes, Mr. Knopp!' ") (3.81).

The vignette on the title page of *Abenteuer eines Junggesellen* had shown a chariot, drawn by two goats and steered by the same cupid who later pulls the curtains of the marital bed. But Knopp, the bachelor, was depicted as being dragged through the dust, his feet tied to the vehicle (Ill. 9). *Herr und Frau Knopp* features a similar conveyance on the title page, but now the new Mrs. Knopp holds the reins and a whip, the smiling cupid sits behind her, and a little cart with a baby in it is attached. The draft animal is Tobias, his coattails twisted together to resemble a horse's tail, and his eyes hidden behind blinders (Ill. 10). This drawing is the backdrop to the first lines of the introductory poem that calls the resolution to get married "lovely," "seemly," and "heartwarming." Matrimony is seen as pleasant and convenient: "Reason as well as sentiment urge marital association" (3.85).

Busch offers a first glance at this cozy relationship when—in solemn dactylic measure, which gives the scene a mock-classical flavor—he describes the start of the day for the newlyweds: "Hier ruht er mit seiner getreuen Dorette / Vereint auf geräumiger Lagerstätte" ("Here he is reposing with his faithful Dorette / United on their spacious resting place") (3.85). After a smile and a kiss, husband and wife engage in a tickling game, but when Tobias tries to escape, Dorothy forcefully pulls him back into bed by the tail of his nightshirt which she twists together like a horse's tail (Ill. 11). The symbolism of the title page that is repeated here throws an ironic light on the next chapter which describes Knopp's daily routine under the heading "Der alte Junge hat's gut" (The Old Boy Is Lucky).

Knopp's day begins with breakfast, which he likes very much, "above all, because it is so comfortable." The maid brings in the breakfast tray, and the master has a chance to tickle her under the chin before turning his grateful and innocent face to his wife who comes in to pour his coffee. He appreciates her special present, a fez to keep his bald head warm, and enjoys his pipe, which she dutifully lights. So the morning passes while lunch is being prepared. Knopp has no reason to complain because his wife's pancakes are excellent. After the meal it is time to get some rest, and he goes to sleep with the words: "Wie schön ist's, Herr Gemahl zu sein!" ("How beautiful it is to be a spouse!") (3.98). Self-satisfied and comfortable, Knopp is not aware of the emptiness of an existence whose highlights are good meals and hours spent in bed or easy chair.

In Munich and in Frankfort, and even in rural Wiedensahl, Busch had studied the counterparts of Tobias Knopp. Egon Friedell commented on the accuracy of his picture of the bourgeois in the age of Bismarck: "What the middle-class German looked like in the second half of the nineteenth century posterity will learn with certainty from *one* master only, Wilhelm Busch. . . . Busch's portraits have an extraordinary cultural-historical value. There he stands before our eyes, the German philistine, with his conventions and crotchets, his daily desires and opinions, his manner of walking, standing, eating, drinking, loving, living, and dying. Caricatured, and yet, strange to say, not in the least distorted; a collective portrait, on which comprehending kindliness has worked as much as keen criticism."[1] The depiction of the German philistine by Heinrich

Mann, George Grosz, Kurt Tucholsky, Erich Kästner, and many others shows that Tobias Knopp did not die when this era came to an end. There are few interruptions of the daily routine in the Knopp household. One source of problems is domestic help. Efficient and attractive Liese is summarily dismissed by Dorothy after Tobias had pinched the maid's leg while she was cleaning the windows. But a succession of replacements proves unsatisfactory, and she is eventually rehired. Another crisis occurs when Tobias, vaguely dissatisfied with all his marital bliss, decides to assert his role as man and master by going to the tavern. When he finally returns home, he faces a series of attacks by malicious objects: pails of water, the open cupboard door, a pitcher of milk, a butter ball, a mousetrap, a bowl of plum jam, all conspire against him. He then finds himself locked out of the bedroom. A very irate Knopp is not pacified the next morning as Dorothy tries to show some affection. He reacts by sweeping the breakfast dishes from the table and calmly emptying his pipe over the broken pieces. Then his wife whispers in his ear and the roaring tyrant becomes a gentle and loving husband.

The last segment of the book reveals what Dorothy's message was—and what the initial vignette had already indicated. Midwife and physician are called, and after a few agonizing hours for Tobias, all ends well: a healthy child lies in the cradle, the happy father has his peace, and the curtain can be drawn.

The opening lines of *Julchen* may be Busch's best-known and most widely quoted couplet: "Vater werden ist nicht schwer, / Vater sein dagegen sehr" ("To become a father is not difficult, / To be a father, however, is very hard") (3. 148). Tobias Knopp has to face this task after overcoming his initial disappointment over the gender of his child. Again, the vignette marks the emphasis: both parents have disappeared from the picture, and the amoretto has laid down bow and arrows in order to support the little girl as she takes her first steps.

But before going into Julie's story, Busch compared in a humorous introduction the attitudes of responsible fathers like Tobias, and of those who might enjoy the pleasures connected with procreation but who are afraid of matrimony. Such an evil person prefers to remain completely wifeless. No "highly esteemed, virtuous superior" watches over him as he "roams about in the world." He runs out of clean shirts, becomes "stooped and wrinkled, ill-tempered, abominable, misshapen" in the end until all females turn away from him:

"Onkel heißt er günst'gen Falles. / Aber dieses ist auch alles" ("At best, he is called 'uncle,' / But that is all there is to it") (3. 148). Behind this funny mask there is Wilhelm Busch, the lifelong bachelor, "roaming about in the world" of Munich, Frankfort, and Wiedensahl. These lines were written during the period of close contact with Johanna Kessler. Her marital status set up a fence that neither was willing to cross. So Busch became "Uncle Wilhelm" to her daughters, Nanda and Letty, and his letters to her start out: "Dear Aunt."

Knopp has to adjust to the new order of things created by the arrival of Julie. As a baby, she demonstrates the basically animalistic nature of the human species by abandoning herself completely to her primitive urges, assuming that "What is pleasing is also permissible; / Because the human being, as a creature, / Does not show a trace of consideration" (3. 151).

Time passes quickly; Julie learns to walk, and her newly acquired mobility and her trend to imitate what she sees lead to a series of minor catastrophes: ink is spilled; her father's watch is broken, her mother's knitting destroyed; a razor serves as a useful tool to remove the tails from a dress coat and the black crust from the tobacco pipe, with the blade losing some of its cutting edge in the process; and her father's top hat substitutes as a chamber pot.

Soon Julie enters school. She already has an eye for boys, but does not find Dieterich Klingebiel, Ferdinand Mickefett, or Peter Sutitt much to her liking. She prefers blond Fritz, the forester's son, who chivalrously comes to her rescue when the others attack her.

Before the parents fully realize it, their daughter has grown up, and her father exclaims in surprise: "The little miss is marriageable!" That prospect poses problems, however. Her four childhood companions are eligible and interested, but none has reached a station in life that Knopp considers adequate. Sutitt is a veterinarian, Mickefett a pharmacist, and Klingebiel a sexton and organist. Fritz, a forester like his father, is the most attractive, but Knopp is concerned about the required dowry in his case. The suitors compete against each other. Sutitt tries to impress Julie with his equestrian skills, but a wasp attack on his horse frustrates his efforts. Klingebiel sings a serenade especially written and composed for her, but Knopp quickly silences him with a gush of water. Mickefett is lured by a note from Julie into her aunt's bedroom, causes a disturbance, and barely manages to escape amidst the havoc so usual in Busch's picture stories.

Julie's heart belongs to handsome Fritz, and when Tobias Knopp discovers them during a nocturnal love scene in the garden, he eventually repeats Charlemagne's generous attitude toward Emma and Eginhard, saying: "Well, you can have each other!!" (3. 202). In the light of the moon, the concluding tableau depicts "a beautiful, touching family scene": daughter and mother embrace to the left, father and son-in-law to the right, and standing erect between the two couples, there is the aunt with a lantern. To add to the perfect symmetry of the picture, Fritz's dachshund occupies the central position at the bottom of this pyramidal composition, sitting up and looking straight at the viewer as if posing for a photograph.

Tobias Knopp, the philistine, has satisfied himself that someone will be "inconvenienced" by his imminent departure. The black Fatal Sister (rendered comical by the giant wart on her nose) can now cut the thread of his life, and the curtain is closed for the last time.

The effect of alcohol on human beings and on animals had always fascinated Busch. In 1878, he devoted an entire book to this theme. The title of this collection, *Die Haarbeutel* (The Hair Bags), goes back to the time of bagwigs, when the merry movements of the hair bag betrayed the wearer's intoxication, or perhaps were reminiscent of the gait of a drunken person. Thus, in North German dialects, the term became synonymous with "tipsy."

This book followed by a few months the last exchange of letters between Busch and Johanna Kessler. The silence between them weighed heavily on him and might account for some of the bitterness of *Die Haarbeutel*. The introductory peom, in which an old man, after finishing a bottle of wine, shares his philosophy with a young listener, presents a pessimistic world view. Despite the humorous elements, we are once again reminded of Schopenhauer: all of life is seen as a chain of suffering. We are born without our consent, and after a short time, we face the enmity of our parents. As we grow up, we try to escape into the world. But the world is filled with people, "especially Jews, women, and Christians," who try to take advantage of us. When we seek pleasure in alcohol, we are soon reminded of the inherent evil of this escape; the mirror shows us what has happened to our noses and bellies, so we should practice abstinence instead: "Enthaltsamkeit ist das Vergnügen / An Sachen, welche wir nicht kriegen" ("Abstinence is the pleasure / Of things which we do not get"). We ought to realize that he who does not need anything has enough (3. 209). Certainly this definition of abstinence is ironic. But determined renunciation of the unattainable was seen by Schopenhauer as a positive attempt to check the overpowering will. In this connection, the philosopher quoted a line from Meister

Eckhart, the medieval mystic, which Busch himself would occasionally cite: "The fastest animal to carry you to perfection is suffering."[2] But it is not hard to see the ironic reference to abstinence as prompted by the relationship with Johanna Kessler.

The picture stories in *Die Haarbeutel* start out in antiquity. In classical elegiacs, Busch narrates how a slightly intoxicated Silenus punished a mischievous Amor. The story concludes: "Heimwärts reitet Silen und spielt auf der lieblichen Flöte, / Freilich verschiedenerlei, aber doch meistens düdellütt!" ("Home is riding Silenus, playing the beautiful panpipe, / Many a tune, to be sure, mostly, however, tweetleetweet!") (3. 217). This tale can be seen as a good-natured spoof of classical mythology, reminiscent of Jacques Offenbach, but there might be a personal message in the humorous story of the love god, forcefully disarmed after shooting his dart, and of Silenus, trying "many a tune" on his instrument, but playing a cheerful chirp most of the time. In his serious poetry, Busch had attempted to offer a different tune, but the audience wanted to be entertained by comic verse and funny drawings.

Most of the other stories in the book also deal with the return home after excessive drinking, but the setting is contemporary rather than classical. The pictures for "Die ängstliche Nacht" (A Fearsome Night) capture with great mastery the visual distortions caused by alcohol. Similarly, in "Der Undankbare" (The Ingrate), the surroundings—as seen by a drunk—are depicted in a graphic style that anticipates Expressionism. The "moral" of this story is dubious: a good Samaritan helps an intoxicated man back to his feet and is mistreated by him in return. In two of the stories alcohol leads to death—as it did in the case of pious Helena. After drinking some kümmel, a young grocer's clerk accidentally pours vitriol instead of schnapps for a customer. He then falls into a barrel of green soap and is suffocated. Mr. Zwiel, in "Eine kalte Geschichte" (A Cold Story), returns home late one winter night, loses his balance, and falls into the rain barrel. With scientific detachment, Busch describes the situation:

> Das Wasser in dem Fasse hier
> Hat etwa null Grad Reaumur.
> Es bilden sich in diesem Falle
> Die sogenannten Eiskristalle.

(The water in the barrel here / Is about zero degrees on the Réaumur scale. / In such case, there is a formation / Of the so-called ice crystals.) (3. 259–60)

Mrs. Pieter, the dairywoman, discovers the dead man in the morning. Mrs. Zwiel's sober reaction is chilling:

> "Schau schau!" ruft sie, in Schmerz versunken,
> "Mein guter Zwiel hat ausgetrunken!
> Von nun an, liebe Madam Pieter,
> Bitt ich nur um ein Viertel Liter!"

("Oh look!" she cries, filled with grief, / "My good Zwiel has had his last drink!/ From now on, my dear Madame Pieter,/ I'll just take a quarter liter!") (3.262)

The title of this picture story obviously refers not only to the outside temperature.

"Vierhändig" (Four-Handed) provides the connection between *Die Haarbeutel* and the book to come out one year later, *Fipps der Affe (Chip the Monkey)*. It is very likely that the short strip grew out of the work done in preparation for that biography of a monkey. After a night of drinking, a man and a monkey wake up on the floor and look at each other with identical facial expressions and gestures, a perfect illustration of Busch's Darwinistic views. In his notes for the text, the author used the name "Jäck" for the monkey, and "Jack" instead of the later "Fipps" occurs in the first sketchy outline for the longer picture story.

In his article of 1878, Paul Lindau had referred to Busch's continuing interest in Dutch and Flemish painting. In an appreciative letter, Busch responded: "I will probably never be able to change my Dutch nature. If you want to sketch in a few lines what happens quickly and springs from natural drives, you will have to concentrate on portraying peasants and animals in action, unless you are a painter of battle pieces. Educated, well-trained people do not show anything" (B, 1.184). The term "well-trained" ("wohldressiert") is significant. Busch did not see an essential difference between the training of animals and the education of human beings. Teaching and training amount to the same attempt at behavior control or modification. Besides depicting "peasants and animals," Busch also enjoyed unmasking "educated, well-trained people." In "Four-Handed," alcohol unites the scholarly master and his monkey on virtually the same level. In *Fipps der Affe*, Dr. Fink and his wife lose their ability to think rationally when a fire breaks out in their home. Instead of rescuing their child, they take bootjack and mousetrap to safety while their monkey fetches the girl and even remembers to pick up the baby's bottle. Professor Klöhn mouths endless platitudes about man's superiority over animals, and about the unique dignity and decorum with which a human being can face any adversity. A moment later, he becomes totally irrational and blind with rage when he discovers that the monkey has filled his hat with ink and put glue on his handkerchief. Busch intensified the comic effect by employing classical meter for the entire scene, leading to Klöhn's ignominious exit: "Hastig begibt er sich fort; indessen die Würde ist mäßig"("Quickly he beats a retreat; but moderate is his decorum") (3.340). The name of the professor is well chosen. "Klönen" is Plattdeutsch for "to chat" or "to talk at length." In the first outline of the story, the Darwinistic satire was even more obvious: he was called "Dr. Monki" (3. 520).

Both "Four-Handed" and *Chip the Monkey* are thus variations of the theme that Busch had already dealt with a few years earlier in a poem in *Kritik des Herzens,* where some solid burghers discuss Darwin's ideas while enjoying their wine. They reject the theory of evolution as being "against human dignity" before stumbling through the door, grunting audibly, and crawling home on all fours (see 2. 513).

In Busch, Darwin's theories are combined with a cultural pessimism that views the "accomplishments" of civilization with skepticism. But—contrary to Rousseau—Busch was far from idealizing "unspoiled nature." Chip the monkey is another of his characters illustrating his interpretation of Schopenhauer's will. When the monkey is introduced in the first chapter, his "activity and enterprising spirit" are called "valuable." If anything goes on anywhere he has to be there. If something pleases him he has to steal it. He imitates everything he sees, and "malice is his favorite subject" (see 3. 276).[3]

Busch was writing this at a time when "activity and enterprising spirit" were widely considered as "valuable." The outcome of the Franco-Prussian War and the creation of the Second Reich had led to an unprecedented economic boom. The "Gründerjahre," the "Years of the Founders," especially the period from 1871 to 1873, had led to the rapid establishment of hundreds of new industrial firms, made possible by the billions that poured into the country as French reparation payments. The German bourgeois looked with pride at the hectic activities all around and at the recent accomplishments in the industrial and technical fields. It was conveniently overlooked, however, that political and social questions demanded solutions ever more urgently.

Busch's animal biography should be seen against this background. Professor Klöhn, in his teleological world view in which everything in nature is designed to enhance man's position, is not just a belated representative of the Enlightenment but rather a spokesman for his society. His humiliation by the monkey is thus symbolic. We can easily understand the mischievous actions of the animal when the professor expounds on the wisdom of nature: animals, so pleasant, harmless, and useful, are wrapped in skins from which boots can be manufactured, and are filled "with meat of quite nutritional value." Despite his intellectual pretentiousness, Klöhn is akin to the African native depicted in the first chapter who tried to catch the monkey in order to eat him, but who suffered painful defeat when his nose ring was attached to a branch by the skillful animal.

Chip is captured by a sailor and sold to Krüll, a barber and hairdresser in Bremen, who is a master in the "art" of making "nice people" out of all customers, whether they have hair or not. He is always busy, and Chip attentively studies his hectic activities. In Krüll's absence, Dümmel, a peasant, enters the shop for a haircut. Chip imitates the master's pace and goes quickly through the motions he has observed. The experience is rather unpleasant for the customer, especially when the scissors not only take off excess hair, but also cut his ear, and when the hot curling iron is applied to the wound. It seems no accident that Busch selected the Darwinian tubercle as the monkey's target. Krüll returns and tries to prevent further damage, but he finds himself literally framed by the most important requisite of his "art," his mirror. After having reduced this workshop of civilization to shambles, Chip moves on to further pranks.

A middle-class home provides the setting for the next scene. Adele and her "soul's companion" are sharing a moment of happiness together, reminiscent of Tobias Knopp's marital bliss. They are about to enjoy the steaming pudding that the gentleman "loves best of all." Their cozy tête-à-tête ends when Chip appears and transforms the pudding into a rather uncomfortable hat for him:

> So wird oft die schönste Stunde
> In der Liebe Seelenbunde
> Durch Herbeikunft eines Dritten
> Mitten durch- und abgeschnitten.

(So the most beautiful hour / Of love's union of souls / Is often cut through and off / By a third party's arrival.) (3. 300)

Chip is caught in a trap which Dr. Fink had set up for the thief of his chickens. Without even looking at his prisoner, the Doctor puts him into a sack and gives him a severe beating before throwing him into an empty chicken coop for the night. His reasoning is that fasting and castigation might be quite refreshing for somebody disinclined toward good deeds (see 3. 309). The draconic measure is enough to transform the impulsive animal into a humble servant. Chip quickly learns how to perform certain household chores and is rewarded for his services by a pair of trousers and a coat. The process of civilizing a beast from the wilderness seems completed. His favorite occupation is watching over the cradle of little Elise. He has also adopted the same tendency toward hypocrisy he has observed in others. Thus, after taking revenge on Jette, the jealous nursemaid who had tricked him, he is resting peacefully as if nothing had happened "and closes his eyes in crafty peace and quiet" (3. 317).

The monkey also has to prove himself in the confrontation with the other animals in the household, Grip the cat, and Snip the dog.[4] The similarity of names suggests that the three are seen as coequals until one emerges as the leader. The two attack him very much as did their counterparts in the earlier short picture story when they turned on Hans Huckebein. Again a stolen bone is the contested object. Like Huckebein, Chip emerges as the undisputed victor, as the fittest to survive, but due to his greater dexterity his counterattack is much more elaborate and forceful, resulting in the partial loss of Grip's tail.

After the Fink home burns down, Chip, the heroic rescuer of little Elise, leads a pampered life. Yet he is restive:

> Denn, leider Gottes, so ist der Schlechte,
> Daß er immer was anderes möchte,
> Auch hat er ein höchst verruchtes Gelüst,
> Grade so zu sein, wie er eben ist.

(For, unfortunately, that is the nature of an evil person, / That he always wants something else, / Also, he has a most wicked desire / To be exactly as he is.) (3. 348)

Chip wants to be "exactly as he is," just as Huckebein would always want to be "the old rascal," even if he lived again. By stripping off his human clothing, the monkey symbolically leaves civilization behind and becomes himself once more. A last short spree of malicious acts follows, leading eventually to a confrontation with Dümmel, who recognizes him as the "confounded barber." The end comes quickly.

Dümmel with his old shotgun, his wife with her broom, and several neighbors—among them the tailor with his scissors and the cobbler with his awl—go after Chip. A shot rings out; the recoil knocks Dümmel and his companions down, setting off Busch's typical chain reaction, with the broom knocking off the tailor's hat, and scissors and awl painfully penetrating the human anatomy. It seems only fitting, in the light of Busch's statement about animals and peasants, that the monkey's nemesis is a peasant whose name speaks for itself: "Dümmel" is derived from *dumm*, "stupid."

A final tableau assembles around the dying animal all those figures who have had contact with him, including the African monkey hunter whose transformation seems similar to that of Chip in the Fink home: as a liveried servant he rides on the carriage in which Adele and her "soul's companion" are traveling. Almost everybody displays the attitude of the villagers following Max and Moritz's death. Only Elise sheds tears over the loss of her companion; the others are happy that their world is intact again.

II *Interlude: For and of Children (1880–1882)*

Fipps der Affe was a book for adults, but author and publisher agreed that the material could be adapted for a picture story for children. Plans were made for a volume containing a hundred pictures to be reproduced in color. Even before the original *Fipps* appeared in print, Busch had completed the text for *Fipps der Affe für Kinder* (Chip the Monkey for Children). Yet the project did not materialize. The technical problems involved in providing color pictures of acceptable quality were greater than anticipated, and Bassermann became concerned about the commercial prospects for a children's book whose production cost would be high. So Busch never drew the necessary pictures.

A comparison of the two monkey stories offers some insight into the distinction Busch saw between a work for mature readers and one for a younger audience. Parts of the original text were incorporated into the new version, but frequently with stylistic changes for easier comprehensibility. There is more direct discourse, and the number of onomatopoetic words is larger. Fewer examples of linguistic grotesque occur, and the verse in general is more reminiscent of *Max und Moritz* than of the later picture stories.

But more significant is the change in emphasis. The ambiguity is reduced that had arisen from focusing simultaneously on cultural criticism and on the manifestation of the unfettered "will" with its selfish maliciousness. Now Chip is punished because he is not ready to mend his evil ways. The reference to his desire to "be exactly as he is" assumes a different meaning as part of a new context in the introductory passage. We learn that Chip's favorite subjects are the deeds of criminals. While it seems for a short period that he has changed and is becoming likable, he is soon his old self again, and eventually has to pay for his wicked deeds (see 3.521). Similarly, Chip's "activity and enterprising spirit" are no longer described as "valuable." He is always active and enterprising in things that will harm others. As a result of this reinterpretation, scenes showing Chip in acts of self-defense are either omitted or modified. The first episode, in which Chip foils the efforts of the monkey catcher, is not included. Probably Busch also felt that the picture of the attacker's nose being twisted into an "anguished spiral," while acceptable to adults because of its grotesque exaggeration, was not suitable for children. Generally there is less violence in this version. Chip's fight with the cat and dog is retained, but in the adaptation the monkey is the aggressor, whereas originally the other two started the quarrel. Those scenes that were critical of contemporary civilization were likewise changed or omitted. No longer is a delicious pudding seen as the culmination of a love relationship. Instead we have a fat man eating by himself. A segment that had satirized the lack of music appreciation in the middle class is eliminated, as is the confrontation with Professor Klöhn.

The children's version of *Fipps der Affe* was the first of a series of works with which Busch tried to appeal to a juvenile audience. While Bassermann was hoping for a repetition of the success of some of the still very popular adult picture stories, Busch's interest moved in a different direction. In October 1881, when he was busy recording the adventures of two boys and their dogs, the author wrote to his publisher: "The new matter on which I am working is slowly growing into a little book for children.—But what else? Well, dear Friend, I have grown old and, to be honest with you: I believe that nothing will be added to the books for grown-ups in the near future" (B, 1.224). That prediction turned out to be wrong, even with respect to the book mentioned. But for the time being the sophisticated humorist and satirical observer of the *petit bourgeois* of the Bismarck era had apparently become a children's author.

We can only speculate about the reasons for Busch's turning away from adult literature. Perhaps a subconscious desire to reach back into the lost world of his "adopted nieces" Nanda and Letty, and through them, into that of his "aunt," their mother, manifested itself. He may have felt impelled to compete with his own—still very popular—*Max und Moritz* and its many imitations.[5] Possibly he also wanted to create something that would be less likely to be misinterpreted.

Stippstörchen für Äuglein und Öhrchen (Small Tales for Little Eyes and Little Ears) appeared in 1880. The word *Stippstörchen* is Low German, and Bassermann suggested that this title, which was incomprehensible for people in Southern Germany, was partly to blame for the disappointing sales figures. But the new title, chosen for the second edition of 1884, *Sechs Geschichten für Neffen und Nichten* (Six Stories for Nephews and Nieces), did not significantly increase public interest in the book. This cool reception must have hurt the author because *Stippstörchen* is obviously a labor of love. Originally, Busch had hoped that the text could be reproduced along with the colored drawings from a hand-lettered design for a more complete integration of verse and picture. But nobody was able to do the lettering to his satisfaction. In order to make the color printing more economical, Bassermann changed the sequence of the stories, much to Busch's displeasure, since the arrangement was far from accidental. Busch wanted to avoid similar color schemes in stories that followed each other immediately. Even more important for him, however, was probably the internal logic of the book.

The first piece in the book is a short lyrical poem about the cheerful robin; it was to have been followed by three fairy tales and three fables in alternating order. But as Bassermann printed it, the initial poem preceded directly the story in which farmer Rüppel kills the rabbit that has just warned him about the wolf. Rüppel's cabbage field is safe now; and for readers bothered by the moral of the tale, Busch added that whoever still asked about the meaning of the incident was obviously as smart as the rabbit was (see 3.394). The unintended contrast between these two introductory items must have been shocking for many. Readers who had expected another *Helene* or *Knopp* were not interested in fairy tales and practical wisdom for children. The subtle drawings and tasteful coloration did not appeal to anybody looking for animal caricatures as *Fipps* had offered them.

Der Fuchs. Die Drachen. Zwei lustige Sachen (The Fox. The Kites. Two Funny Stories) came out a year later and was equally unsuccessful. The rhymed title shows that the book was designed as a companion volume to its predecessor. This time, the author was able to integrate text and picture. He did the lettering himself, and the thirty-six pages of the volume came close to his concept of a total work of art (Ill. 12). But the formal artistry and technical perfection do not make up for the relative paucity of ideas in those two picture stories. After the imaginative treatment of the confrontation between humans and animals in "Hans Huckebein" and *Fipps der Affe*, the fruitless attempts of a peasant to kill the fox he has trapped seem dull. The simple morality of the tale of three boys who want to fly their kites is closer to *Struwwelpeter* than to *Max und Moritz*: good Conrad is rewarded by seeing his kite fly higher and higher; his companions are punished for stealing apples.

In his desire to write for children, Busch also sacrificed some of the originality and freshness of his poetic language. His verse flows easily but, viewing the verbal excitement of some of the earlier books, the text is a disappointment. Yet, this work is of significance, as Bohne asserts, "because it reflects the psychological situation of a great artist at the calm apex of his life's orbit, a work created immediately before a psychological and physical crisis that preceded the ascent to the actual summit of all his picture stories" (3.531). In February 1881, Busch came down with nicotine poisoning, a condition that was to recur in the fall. In March he went to Munich for his last visit. He returned to Wiedensahl very abruptly after causing a disturbance during the performance of a hypnotist. The incident occurred three days before he turned forty-nine, and his letters from this period show that he felt he had reached old age.

Perhaps Busch had originally conceived of *Plisch und Plum* (Plish and Plash) as one more book for children. But instead it became another best-selling picture story for adults. The alliterating title marks a turning away from the two previous publications and is reminiscent of "Hans Huckebein" and *Max und Moritz*. This connection does not seem accidental. In "Hans Huckebein," one boy and his malicious animal were presented; *Max und Moritz* featured two bad boys; in this latest book, two boys are coupled with two unruly animals. But there are important differences. In the earlier works, the evildoers had to pay with their lives for disturbing the peace of the bourgeois world, whereas in *Plisch und Plum*, the two boys as well as their dogs become pillars of society through the power of education. Max and Moritz were ground up in the mill of justice; Paul and Peter are depicted at the end of the book in their Sunday finery, looking very much like Conrad, the good little boy whose kite flew so high.

Max and Moritz had started out by causing the death of Widow Bolte's poultry, whereas Paul and Peter are shown in the first chapter as the rescuers of two puppies. Max and Moritz were active perpetrators of malicious pranks; Paul and Peter, for the most part, are interested bystanders.

Busch's canine story seems more carefully constructed than most of his earlier works. A circular pattern could be observed in *Max und Moritz*, where the two boys first fed and then ate the birds and eventually were themselves transformed into feed for the birds. Now the pattern is even more pronounced: the first scene takes place at the pond where old Kaspar Schlich tries to drown his unwanted puppies. The book ends with Schlich drowning in the same pond after witnessing how Plish and Plash brought unexpected financial gains to their new owners. In the intervening chapters, he had made his appearance to give spiteful comments whenever the two dogs had done some damage. Busch's frequent use of refrain finds a culmination here. In *Max und Moritz*, every chapter had concluded with a variation of the same ominous statement: "Dieses war der erste Streich, / Doch der zweite folgt sogleich" ("This was their first prank, / But the second one will follow at once") (1.349). Each episode of Tobias Knopp's search for a wife had concluded in a similar fashion: "Schnell verläßt er diesen Ort / Und begibt sich weiter fort" ("He quickly leaves this place / And proceeds further on") (3.18). Each maid was dismissed by Mrs. Knopp with the same words: "Sie ruft: 'Das bitt ich mir aber aus!/ Abscheuliches Mädchen, verlasse das Haus!' " ("She shouts: 'I must insist!/ Disgusting girl, leave the house!' ") (3.101). While in these instances the refrain was used to indicate the repetitiveness of the situation, in *Julchen* it is employed to suggest the rapid passage of time: "Einszweidrei, im Sauseschritt, / Läuft die Zeit; wir laufen mit" ("Onetwothree, with rushing pace, / Time is racing; we race along") (3.155). Here the refrain is also translated into a graphic image: the text is accompanied in each instance by the identical vignette of a running figure, with hourglass and scythe, rendered grotesque by being clad in a skirt or nightgown and a bed jacket, while the head is hidden in the clouds (Ill. 13).

In Kaspar Schlich's refrainlike appearances, his words, in each case illustrated by a drawing of his face with the appropriate expression, bring his character into clearer focus. He becomes the embodiment of *Schadenfreude*, of spiteful glee at the misfortunes of others. When the dogs ruin the supper Mother Fittig has prepared, when they

chew up the boys' trousers and shoes, when they destroy a neighbor's
flower bed and soil her laundry, when they attack Shmul Schiefelbeiner and tear his clothing, when they create havoc in the kitchen
and cause a fight between the two boys, Schlich's reaction is
invariably the same: " 'Ist fatal!'—bemerkte Schlich—/'Hehe! aber
nicht für mich!' " (" 'That's unfortunate!'—observed Schlich—/
'Heehee! but not for me!' ") (3.469) (Ill. 14). But when he voices his
glee after the dogs have upset the container with pancake batter, the
angry Father Fittig slaps a hot pancake over his head. This time
Schlich has to modify his comment: " 'Most unfortunate!'—observed
Schlich—/'But this time also for me!' " (3.498). And when an English
tourist buys the two dogs for a large sum of money, Schlich has one
last statement before his envy kills him: " 'Rather pleasing!'—he
murmurs—/ 'But unfortunately not for me!!' " (3.513).

The skillful grouping of the principal characters of the story is
another indication of Busch's careful planning: the physical traits of
the parents are reflected in their sons. Father Fittig is tall and very
lean, and Paul shows the same features, complete with pointed nose
and tuft of hair. Mother Fittig is short and plump, and Peter
represents the identical type. Each boy selects a canine companion
strikingly similar to him. The names they give their dogs are
onomatopoetic and related to the animals' physical differences: when
Schlich throws the puppies into the pond, the slender one glides in
smoothly, while the plump one hits the water with an audible and
visible splash.[6]

The secondary characters in the story indicate clearly that *Plisch
und Plum* is a book for adults. As has been suggested, there is
something "sadistically perverted" in the image of the very proper
Madame Kümmel, dousing the dogs' raised backsides with kerosene
as they are digging into her flower bed in pursuit of a mouse,
especially since Busch describes her as acting "angrily, but with
enjoyment."[7] The Schiefelbeiner episode has occasionally been cited
as another example of Busch's anti-Semitism. Yet, as in the similar
description in *Die fromme Helene*, Busch is far from giving a realistic
portrait, but presents a caricature of the middle-class Christian image
of the Jew, with his short pants, his long coat, his crooked nose and
cane, his black eyes, his grey soul, and his sly mien. As if wanting to
make quite sure that nobody overlooked the irony, Busch added a
parenthetical statement: "Schöner ist doch unsereiner!" ("Our kind is
certainly more beautiful!") (3. 479). No readers familiar with Busch's

work could accept this as his serious opinion. Quite in line with this societal prejudice against the Jew, Paul and Peter condone their dogs' attack on Schiefelbeiner. His request for compensation for his torn pants, and his threat to sue in case his demand is not met, appear completely justified. Ironically, Fittig displays the attitude toward money that gentile bias normally associates with the Jew: "Er muß zahlen. —Und von je / Tat ihm das doch gar so weh" ("He has to pay. —And all his life / That has always hurt him very much") (3.484). Consequently, when Mr. Pief, the eccentric Englishman, offers him a hundred marks for the two dogs that have retrieved his hat and telescope, Fittig is very happy to accept the money which he has done nothing to earn: "Er fühlt sich wie neugestärkt, / Als er so viel Geld bemerkt" ("He feels as if newly strengthened / When he notices that much money") (3.512).

The English tourist is another caricature designed to appeal to adult sophistication even though children might also delight in his grostesqueness. Like a Phileas Fogg, lifted from the pages of Jules Verne and transplanted to the North German marshlands, he is undaunted by all adversities, including his fall into the pond caused by his habit of looking through his telescope rather than watching his way (Ill. 15).

The view of education presented in this picture story is worthy of analysis, especially when compared with some of Busch's earlier works. Peter and Paul are directly or indirectly responsible for considerable damage done by their pets. But in each case they appear quite unperturbed. Thus Father Fittig, becoming yet another of Busch's spokesmen for the primacy of evil over good, decides that his sons need supervision: " 'Dies'—denkt er—'muß anders werden!/ Tugend will ermuntert sein, / Bosheit kann man schon allein!' " (" 'This'—he thinks—'has to change!/ Virtue has to be encouraged, / Malice one can do by oneself!' ") (3. 499). The instrument of change is Master Bokelmann, the teacher, who begins by making a little speech in rather quaint language to the amused rascals. It is significant that the value of education is described by him purely in terms of social prestige and material gains, and that politeness is defined as an attitude that will stave off unpleasant situations.

After outlining his educational ideals he expresses hope that the boys will promise to mend their ways. But they display the same attitude as Kuno Debisch after his father's stern exhortation. So Bokelmann immediately applies Druff's method by giving them a severe caning. That changes their attitudes very drastically. When he asks his "beloved boys" whether they are contented and in agreement with him, they quickly assure him of their cooperation. The next picture shows the effectiveness of the procedure: Paul and Peter, neatly dressed, look like perfect miniaturized adults:

> Dies ist Bokelmanns Manier.
> Daß sie gut, das sehen wir.
> Jeder sagte, jeder fand:
> "Paul und Peter sind scharmant!!"

(This is Bokelmann's way. / We can see that it is good. / Everybody said, everybody felt:/"Paul and Peter are charming!!") (3. 506)

This positive assessment obviously represents the view of the adult majority. The two boys have been beaten into submission; they have adapted to the conditions of the grown-up world, and their angelic smiles indicate that they have mastered the hypocrisy necessary to get ahead in their society. By being polite to everybody, they will avoid future annoyances. The fact that they can take leave of Plish and Plash so easily when money is offered clearly shows that they have left childhood behind. It says something about the *Zeitgeist* that in 1910 Fritz Winther could call Bokelmann a teacher after Busch's own heart, the only capable educator ever portrayed by the author.[8]

The boys apply Bokelmann's method to their canine friends, and once again the basic identity of human education and animal training is demonstrated:

> Bald sind beide kunstgeübt,
> Daher allgemein beliebt,
> Und, wie das mit Recht geschieht,
> Auf die Kunst folgt der Profit.

(Soon both are quite skilled in their arts, / Therefore generally popular, / And, as that so rightly happens: / Art is followed by profit.) (3.507)

This reference to art and profit should give any reader pause who might be inclined to take the view on education presented here too seriously. The theme of art and profit and, more broadly, the role of art and literature in the bourgeois society was once again to be touched upon in Busch's next books.

III   *The Bourgeois as Artist: The Artist as Bourgeois (1883–1884)*

Throughout his life, Wilhelm Busch identified with the class he so often satirized in word and picture, the bourgeoisie. In his last two picture stories, the culmination of his work in this genre, he dealt with the theme of the "bourgeois who strayed off into art" twenty years before Thomas Mann's *Tonio Kröger*. As in Mann, some personal experience can be traced in the work. But the very names of Busch's protagonists indicate ironic distancing. How can a Balduin Bählamm (Baldwin Baalamb) be expected to produce great literature? What masterpieces will be painted by Kuno Klecksel whose name is derived from *Klecks*—"blot" or "blotch"?

Balduin Bählamm, der verhinderte Dichter (Baldwin Baalamb, Poet Manqué—or, more literally, the Prevented Poet) was published in the summer of 1883. The long introductory poem sets the tone. A poet's privileged position is ironically described: "Wie wohl ist dem, der dann und wann / Sich etwas Schönes dichten kann!" ("How fine he feels, who every now and then / Can write himself some beautiful poetry!") (4.7). Many people are unhappy in life and do not know how to cope with the world. But if the poet dislikes this "stale world," he "kneads from soft bran" his own private one. So poetry serves as an escape from harsh reality. The nutritional image of "soft bran" leads to an even more drastic metaphor: the poet's material runs in constant flow from the "motherly bosoms" of the "eternally well-nourished Muses" into his "clean dairy." Busch describes a farmer's wife who, after milking her cows, proceeds to work on the liquid thus obtained until the "tortured element," "out of fear," starts to "separate into thick and thin." This is the moment of bliss: she takes the part that has thickened and kneads it into a shapely ball of butter. "Just so the poet," who, like the farmer's wife, wants to share with others that whose production has given him so much joy. How beautiful it is if the result of the poet's thinking and feeling is published in the morning paper! People can enjoy it with their coffee and fresh rolls. Everybody will say: "What a charming poem!" But even greater reward awaits him when his Laura flies into his arms, whispering that she is giving her heart to the "divine man" because he can write so nicely (see 4.7–10).

The next chapter introduces the hero: "Ein guter Mensch, der Bählamm hieß / Und Schreiber war, durchschaute dies" ("A good man, whose name was Baalamb, / And who was a clerk, recognized

this") (4.11). We already know that his efforts are doomed. The
drastic comparisons of the introduction, and the concept of poetry
and creativity presented there make it clear, however, that his failure
may be sad for him, but that it will not be tragic.
   Baalamb has a secure position in his office, is married, and has
already fathered four children. But he feels a "deep longing" to
"expand his happiness even further." He wants to write verse in
order to "give himself and others joy": "Er fühlt, er muß und also
kann es" ("He feels, he must, and thus he can do it") (4.11). Baalamb
never has an opportunity to demonstrate his presumed ability to
"give himself and others joy," since the world seems to have
conspired to prevent him from kneading his "ball of butter." When he
looks for a "solemn spot" to sit down, since he is "full of feeling and
heavy with thought," all park benches are already occupied. He finds
an empty table in a beer garden and is just ready to jot down a brilliant
idea when a "friend with a good sense of humor" approaches him from
behind and knocks his hat over his head. Filled with indignation,
Baalamb goes home, where he takes off hat and coat,

> Und schmückt in seinem Kabinett
> Mit Joppe sich und Samtbarett,
> Die, wie die Dichtung Vers und Reim,
> Den Dichter schmücken, der daheim.

(And adorns himself, in his cabinet, / With jacket and with velvet barret, /
Which, just as verse and rhyme do for poetry, / Decorate the poet who is at
home.) (4.17)

These lines are a telling commentary on his attitude toward poetic
creativity. A change in clothing is required for the metamorphosis
from clerical worker to literary artist. The old-fashioned velvet
headgear sets him visibly apart from ordinary human beings.[9] The
bourgeois becomes an artist by dressing according to his conception
of an artist's appearance. His understanding of what constitutes the
essence of poetry is just as superficial: rhyme and verse are mere
decorations which, when added to a prosaic statement, turn it into
lyrical poetry.
   Baalamb's home does not provide any better conditions for creative
work than did the public park or the beer garden. The carefully
excluded brutal reality intrudes repeatedly. But "a great mind like
Baalamb's" has an answer. He decides to leave for the country. There
"honesty is not yet out of date," and "quiet reigns and peace prevails"

(4.23). Even if we were not familiar with Busch's depiction of the "country" as the realm of Max and Moritz, and of peasants named Dümmel or Rüppel, we could assume that Baalamb will not find what he expects.

The would-be poet tries to utilize the train journey to compose some verse, but just as the "most beautiful thoughts" finally occur to him, he arrives at his destination. He tries to leave the car when a fat man with heavy nailed shoes squeezes in. He steps on Baalamb's toe, and Busch assumes once again his stance as a cool, scientific observer. At the same time, he provides some insight into the mechanism of *Schadenfreude*:

> Des Lebens Freuden sind vergänglich;
> Das Hühnerauge bleibt empfänglich.
> Wie dies sich äußert, ist bekannt.
> Krumm wird das Bein und krumm die Hand;
> Die Augenlöcher schließen sich,
> Das linke ganz absonderlich;
> Dagegen öffnet sich der Mund,
> Als wollt er flöten, spitz und rund.
> Zwar hilft so eine Angstgebärde
> Nicht viel zur Lindrung der Beschwerde;
> Doch ist sie nötig jederzeit
> Zu des Beschauers Heiterkeit.

(The joys of life are fleeting; / The corn remains receptive. / It is well known how this manifests itself. / The leg is bent, and bent the hand; / The eye apertures close, / Particularly the left one; / On the other hand, the mouth opens, / As if to whistle, pointed and round. / Such a gesture of anxiety / Does little to alleviate the discomfort, to be sure, / But it is always necessary / For the observer's amusement.) (4.28–29)

The village is deceptively peaceful. Jörg, the little boy, is happily riding his hobbyhorse through the mud. Krischan Bopp, the farmer, is enjoying his pipe while standing on his "cozy dunghill," watching pretty Rieke Mistelfink cleaning her goat stall. Within a short time, all of them will join forces to frustrate Baalamb's poetic efforts.

The setting for the first attempt to write seems propitious. Seated at an open window, Baalamb abandons himself to the mood created by the sunset and the sound of cowbells. He is ready to write down the first verse when a bovine head comes through the window and "bawls like a trombone" into his ear. The "power of harsh sounds" causes "verse and rhyme to become unglued." In light of the milk-and-butter metaphor, it is ironic that a cow is thus responsible for the first disruption of the creative process.

After a restless night, Baalamb decides to write outdoors, under the blooming lilac. This gives young Jörg a chance to demonstrate his malicious inventiveness. By means of a pin, he fashions an effective weapon from his hobbyhorse. Hidden behind a fence, he pricks his victim with the pin, snatches away his hat, and removes his chair, so that Baalamb sits down in the nettles. An attempt by the poor man to grasp at the stick results in his hand being punctured by the pin, and a cheerful Jörg continues on his way.

The poet seeks seclusion and inspiration as far away from civilization as possible:

> In freier Luft, in frischem Grün,
> Da, wo die bunten Blümlein blühn,
> In Wiesen, Wäldern, auf der Heide,
> Entfernt von jedem Wohngebäude,
> Auf rein botanischem Gebiet,
> Weilt jeder gern, der voll Gemüt.
> Hier legt sich Bählamm auf den Rücken
> Und fühlt es tief und mit Entzücken,
> Nachdem er Bein und Blick erhoben:
> Groß ist die Welt, besonders oben!

(In open air, in nature's freshness, / Where colorful little flowers bloom, / In meadows, forests, heathland, / Far from any residential building, / In a purely botanic area, / That's where anybody full of feeling likes to be. / This is where Baalamb lies down on his back / And feels deeply and with delight, / After having lifted one leg and his eyes:/ The world is great, especially above!) (4.42)

Peter Marxer has called attention to the similarity of this passage with the letter of May 10 in Goethe's *Werther*.[10] Both Werther and Baalamb revel in the beauty of a romanticized nature; both lack the discipline or true creativity to translate their enthusiasm into works of art. Yet the differences between the two men are more significant than their similarities. Baalamb would never be driven to suicide. Goethe had Werther speak to the reader directly through his letters, whereas Busch served as an intermediary between his protagonist and the reader. His realistic world view results in an ironic alienation that makes his work appear like a deliberate parody of *Werther*. Goethe's hero, when lying in the grass, feels the "breath of the

All-loving One" and longs for the ability to transfer onto paper what is so fully and warmly alive within him, so that it might become the mirror of his soul, just as his soul is the mirror of infinite God.[11] The banality of Baalamb's insight presents a striking contrast. Werther had written: "I feel this teeming little world among the stalks closer to my heart—the countless, unfathomable forms of tiny worms and gnats—and feel the presence of the Almighty." Busch gives very concrete shape to these "unfathomable forms of tiny worms": an earwig selects Baalamb's ear as a comfortable resting place, thereby quickly bringing the poet back from his dreams into reality. Linguistically, Busch sets his hero clearly apart from Werther whose enthusiastic *Sturm und Drang* language is stylistically uniform. In *Balduin Bählamm,* the romantic mood evoked by much of the vocabulary is broken by the incorporation of words from a completely different, prosaic level of language, such as "residential buildings" or "purely botanical area."

Baalamb's encounters continue to be unhappy. An attempt to present a nosegay to Rieke results in a powerful box on the ear. Busch describes again with scientific detachment what happens when the hand, filled with energy that is transformed into swinging motion as the result of excitement, meets with the cheek where energy becomes heat. This heat, then, through inflammation of nerves, is felt as painful sensation: "Ohrfeige heißt man diese Handlung,/ Der Forscher nennt es Kraftverwandlung" (" 'Box on the ear' is the name of this action,/ The scientist calls it 'transformation of energy' ") (4.52).

Baalamb tries one last time to compose some verse, inspired by the atmosphere of the village resting in the moonlight. Suddenly Rieke, who seems to have forgotten her earlier behavior, beckons from an open window. He eagerly follows the invitation and, after squeezing through the narrow window, finds himself in the company of an aggressive goat rather than a love-starved maiden. A big basket, into which he rushes headfirst, offers some protection against the animal's sharp horns. Rieke and her lover Krischan find Baalamb's position quite convenient as they pick up the container and carry it to a nearby pond. After dunking him several times, his tormentors empty their basket into the cool water and return home in complete happiness.

A severe toothache is the consequence of the unexpected cold bath. Dr. Schmurzel, the dentist, is cheerful as always when someone else feels pain. His unsuccessful efforts to extract the tooth cause further agony. While great lyrical poets certainly need the experience of profound pain—Busch's ironic comment—an ordinary pain such as Baalamb's hardly propels a writer into the pantheon.

The hapless "prevented poet" returns home and goes to bed in exhaustion. While his toothache subsides, he has a beautiful dream vision. On pink clouds a winged lady in white appears, smiling and beckoning him to join her. The drawing shows her features as those of Rieke Mistelfink. Miraculously, the dreamer has sprouted wings and is ready to rise up for a blissful union when he feels himself pulled down by a heavy weight. Again the accompanying picture is a necessary complement to the text. It shows that his wife and his children constitute the burden. The heavenly phenomenon fades away, a goat bleats mockingly, and Baalamb hears his wife's voice telling him that it is time to get up. At nine o'clock, he walks to his office as always. As so often, Busch concludes with a statement in which a banality is presented as if it were the most profound wisdom:

> So steht zum Schluß am rechten Platz
> Der unumstößlich wahre Satz:
> Die Schwierigkeit ist immer klein,
> Man muß nur nicht verhindert sein.

(Here is, in conclusion, in its proper place, / The irrefutably true doctrine: / The difficulty is always small, / As long as one is not prevented.) (4.80)

The final picture shows the "prevented poet" on his way to work, weighed down under the load of "small difficulties" that have kept him from reaching his goal (Ill. 16). The contrast with the first picture of Baalamb is especially striking. There he was shown, pen behind ear and eyes lifted, in expectation of immediate divine inspiration (Ill. 17). This portrait had been preceded, however, by the title vignette of a crying little cherub with his wings tied together.

Maler Klecksel (Blotty the Painter) appeared exactly one year after *Balduin Bählamm*. Thematically as well as in format, the two picture stories belong together. Again Busch sets the tone for his biography of a bourgeois artist in a long introductory poem. But while he had addressed himself immediately to the theme of poetry in the opening lines of the earlier book, the route is more circuitous this time. First he discusses the salutary function of talking for man, "provided he does it for himself." The metaphor used shows how much Busch was a painter at heart, translating ideas into visual images: human thoughts are seen as a fleet of sailboats, gaily passing through the opened lock gates of the mouth, traveling—if the wind is favorable—on the waves of sound to the ports of the ears of the listener, those "well-known open spaces." The politician is a master in the skill of talking, making people accept as truth whatever he says. Others, lacking his ability and self-assurance, might opt to talk about art instead. It is easy to speak about this topic, especially if one does not understand anything about it. Instead of literary teas, or concerts where the grunting and whining of instruments make talking difficult, the "quiet world of the paintbrush" is to be preferred. The speaker likes to spend his afternoons—of course mostly in the company of ladies—in the art gallery, the "realm of gilded frames." Beauty and taste rule here; it smells pleasantly of varnish; and walls do not have to go naked because magnificent paintings in all sizes dress them up and quietly wait to be appreciated (4.83). The superficiality of this concept of art parallels Baalamb's idea of poetry. But Baalamb had viewed poetry as an escape from his middle-class routine, whereas now art is seen through the eyes of the bourgeoisie as part of its world. The creative artist is perceived as an interior decorator. It is quite logical that the "appreciation" of the work of art is based on its price tag.

Art embellishes this world. The architect deserves our respect for adorning the coarse and sooty crust of our old earth with clean buildings, towers, and barracks. The sculptor gives us pleasure by putting up monuments of great men everywhere, so that a traveler can feel at home in any strange town when he sees the well-known statue of Schiller in front of the railroad station. But even greater is the painter's glory, for he makes our world colorful. He puts world history on the walls of public halls, he furnishes humorous or touching genre pictures; he creates green landscape paintings, tavern signs, and coats of arms; and he has—for a thousand years or less—preserved our ancestry in oil. Busch's satire is obvious, and before we have even met the protagonist of the story we have learned not to take his art seriously. The materialistic aspect of art in this society is further stressed in the passage leading into the actual life story of Kuno Klecksel: young men are encouraged to "throw themselves into painting"—perhaps they can even earn money that way (see 4.84).

The title vignette shows Kuno with palette and paintbrush, ready to work (Ill. 18). But the interior vignette prepares us for the upshot of his artistic career: a cheerful little devil, stepping out of an overturned beer stein, is sweeping the palette clean with a broom. He seems about to sweep away the poor painter himself who lies helpless

on his back (Ill. 19). However, we are only at the beginning of his
curriculum vitae, and Busch, returning again to the refrain
technique, concludes the introduction with a couplet that recurs with
the appropriate modifications at the end of each of the following nine
chapters: "Nach diesem ermunterungsvollen Vermerke / Fahren wir
fort im löblichen Werke" ("After this encouraging note, / We will
continue in our laudable work") (4.84).

Chubby little Kuno is a normal baby. The "worldly little philistine"
loves his bottle and is fascinated by the light effects produced by the
candle: his future career seems already indicated. As a boy, he enjoys
drawing, but when he enters school, Mr. Bötel, his teacher, is no
admirer of his art, especially when it manifests itself in a caricature on
the blackboard. The angry educator punishes Kuno, who takes his
revenge by setting off a homemade explosive device under the
teacher's window late at night, and by squirting the frightened man
with animal blood from a syringe. After Bötel realizes that he is still
alive, steps are taken to reform Kuno, but—like Huckebein and
Chip—he is destined to remain what he is:

> Wenn wer sich wo als Lump erwiesen,
> So bringt man in der Regel diesen
> Zum Zweck moralischer Erhebung
> In eine andere Umgebung.
> Der Ort ist gut, die Lage neu.
> Der alte Lump ist auch dabei.

(If somebody somewhere has proved to be a scoundrel, / He is, as a rule, / For
the purpose of moral elevation, / Taken to different surroundings. / The place
is good, the situation new. / The old scoundrel is there, too.) (4.94)

Quast, the house painter, provides the new surroundings. His
apprentice is not very eager to learn his trade. Instead, he uses his
master's expensive paint to decorate stray dogs. When he is punished
by being deprived of food, he decides to leave for the "City of the
Muses," but not before combining various household articles into a
monument to his departure and transforming Quast into a birdlike
creature by cutting open his feather quilt and pouring a bottle of
varnish over the sleeper.

Kuno's new residence is obviously modeled after Munich, the art
metropolis Busch knew so well; and he appears to have incorporated
much of his own experience into this story. Certainly he himself had
encountered the attitudes toward art that are satirized in the
introductory poem. But while Kuno's adventures as an art student

are, in part, based on Busch's observations in Düsseldorf, Antwerp, and Munich, the autobiographical aspects of this picture story should not be overemphasized. Kuno Blotty is another "imaginary Jack" and should not be confused with his creator.

Busch may have thought of the relationship with his father when he drafted the letter in which Kuno informs his family that he is now an art student and needs money. The image of the father, scraping the sum together and warning his son not to be wasteful seems an echo of the years when young Wilhelm had to rely on parental support. Kuno is relieved of his financial worries for the time being and can devote himself to his chosen field. He soon excels in his art class, doing well in skills like sharpening pencils and brushing with the eraser. "When it comes to hachure, which is the hardest, he is absolutely ahead of all" (4.108). So he can soon progress to the hall of antiques where he happily draws the statues of somewhat defective gods and goddesses. Female figures are especially pleasing to him. The aspiring young painter is successful only in the purely mechanical aspects of his profession, and his work in the hall of antiques gives little evidence of artistic genius. This ironic account assumes special significance when we compare it with Busch's summary of his disappointing experience in Düsseldorf: "After having lived in Hanover for three or four years, I betook myself to the Düsseldorf hall of antiques, encouraged by a painter. By means of applying eraser, white bread, and chalk, I practiced and mastered there the popular method of stippling through which one produces the lovely lithographic 'grain'" (4.149).

There are other pleasures for Kuno besides sketching classical sculptures. On nice summer afternoons, he leaves his work, "Und eilt mit brennender Havanna / Zum Schimmelwirt zu der Susanna" ("And hurries, with his Havana burning, / To the White Horse Tavern and to Susan") (4.110). As Kraus notes, hte perfect harmony of rhyme, rhythm, and meaning in this case combines cigar, tavern, and waitress into the quintessence of middle-class well-being.[12] This bourgeois idyll lasts only until Kuno's money runs out, which occurs earlier than expected, due to his greatly increased consumption of beer. A whole chapter deals with his unsuccessful attempts to borrow some money from his well-to-do friend Gnatzel, who skillfully avoids any situation that might give Kuno a chance to make his request.

In desperation, Kuno tries to utilize his artistic talents to improve his financial situation. Since historical pictures are popular, he tries his hand at a portrait of the inventor of gunpowder two seconds after his great discovery. Busch's drawing complements the text: the traces of the obviously unexpected explosion are all over the poor monk. Unfortunately, it proves easier to produce a picture than to sell it. Kuno's chances of finding a buyer are further decreased by a devastating critique in the newspaper authored by Dr. Hinterstich, whose name means "stab from behind." The enraged painter rushes to the critic's office, and a violent struggle ensues. Hinterstich uses his pen and his inkwell as weapons; Kuno attacks him with his umbrella and, after having gained the upper hand, employs his pencil to emphasize once more the meaning of his opponent's name. The victor leaves the scene with his umbrella raised in the triumphant gesture so often to be found in Busch's drawings.[13] The moral is clear: "Ein rechter Maler, klug und fleißig, /Trägt stets 'n spitzen Bleistift bei sich" ("A real painter, smart and diligent, / Always carries a sharpened pencil along") (4.126).

Kuno is fortunate to find a patron in Fräulein von der Ach, an aging spinster. He had come to her rescue when she was being dragged through the dirt by two big dogs in whose leash she had become entangled. In gratitude, she orders a painting of a "somehow legendary" subject and makes a handsome advance payment. The young man decides to illustrate the ballad of "The Dauntless Knight and the Horrible Dragon," probably a remnant of Busch's Jung-München club journal contributions. The young painter's lack of artistic vision becomes obvious:

> Gar oft erfreut das Fräulein sich
> An Kunos kühnem Kohlenstrich,
> Obgleich ihr eigentlich nicht klar,
> Wie auch dem Künstler, was es war.

(Very often the Fräulein delighted / In Kuno's bold charcoal stroke, / Even though it was actually not clear to her, / Nor to the artist, what it represented.) (4.135)

Especially the portrayal of the rescued maiden presents problems due to the lack of an appropriate model. His patroness immediately offers her services, but Kuno forgets all about their appointment when he goes to the carnival costume ball with Susan, whose faithful devotion to him has been restored now that he has money again. The Munich artists' balls probably provided the model for the description of the festivities attended by the painter and the waitress, dressed as elegant cavalier and innocent shepherdess (since during carnival everybody tries very hard to appear as that which he is not). They

retire to his studio after the dance. When the eager model arrives at the appointed time, Susan quickly hides, but is discovered, and the indignant would-be patroness leaves the studio for good. After this adventure, Busch brings the "laudable work" rather abruptly to a close.
The brief final chapter of the story starts with some philosophical observations. Beneath the casual language and the humorous metaphors, we get a glimpse of the aging author whose close friend Lorenz Gedon in Munich had just died of cancer, and who was engaged in an ongoing discussion of religion and man's position in the universe with Hermann Levi, who was considering conversion from Judaism. There is another echo of Schopenhauer's concept of the destruction of individuality in death, while life as "will" is certain to surface again:

> Hartnäckig weiter fließt die Zeit;
> Die Zukunft wird Vergangenheit.
> Von einem großen Reservoir
> Ins andre rieselt Jahr um Jahr;
> Und aus den Fluten taucht empor
> Der Menschen buntgemischtes Korps.
> Sie plätschern, traurig oder munter,
> 'n bissel 'rum, dann gehen's unter
> Und werden, ziemlich abgekühlt,
> Für längre Zeit hinweggespült.—
> Wie sorglich blickt das Aug' umher!
> Wie freut man sich, wenn der und der,
> Noch nicht versunken oder matt,
> Den Kopf vergnügt heroben hat.

(Time is stubbornly flowing on;/ Future turns into past./ Year after year is running / From one great reservoir into another;/ And from the flood there is emerging / The motley corps of human beings./ They splash around a little, sad or cheerful, / And then they go under / And are, quite cooled off, / Flushed away for a longer period of time.—/ How anxiously one's eyes are looking about!/ How happy one is if this person or that,/ Not yet submerged or weary, /Is cheerfully keeping his head up.) (4.143)

The story ends on a conciliatory note. The "stubborn flow of time" has brought about the decease of the old owner of the White Horse Tavern, and the new one, Kuno Blotty, is happily announcing to the world that his wife Susan just gave birth to their fifth son. Except for Fräulein von der Ach, who, "in angry resignation," has entered a convent, all of Kuno's former adversaries are united in a final tableau, enjoying their brew in his beer garden. Quast, Gnatzel, and even Hinterstich nod their agreement, as Bötel says with conviction: "Where would we be without the right kind of education?" Perhaps Busch knew that he had finished his last picture story when he wrote: "After this note by Bötel / We cheerfully conclude the laudable work" (4.145).

Certainly this ending is more "cheerful" than the drawing of Baldwin Baalamb on his way to work. Busch seems to have made his peace with the world and with himself. But we should remember that the happy beer drinkers represent the philistine and materialistic world view of Tobias Knopp, Uncle Nolte, and Böck the tailor. The "right kind of education" referred to is the same type that Lämpel and Master Bokelmann supply. The men in Blotty's tavern have learned to function as useful members of their society, quite happy within the confines of their societal roles and with their limited vision. While Baalamb is crushed, he had at least tried to leave his bourgeois existence temporarily for what he naively considered to be the realm of art. Kuno Blotty, however, has readily given up all pretenses of being an artist for the privilege of a middle-class life that enables him to satisfy his thirst for beer without having to worry about the money. Busch had long ago decided to abandon his envisioned career as a painter because he realized his own limitations and was not willing to compromise. In Kuno's case, that step was taken in order to insure a comfortable existence. It was, after all, the bottle and not the candle that had attracted the "worldly little philistine" first.

CHAPTER 4

Romanticism Versus Realism: Busch's Poetry

I Critique of the Heart (*1874*)

IN the early 1870s, there were persistent rumors that the popular
picture stories were in effect a joint production by Wilhelm
Busch, who provided the drawings, and a brother of his, who
furnished the text. It was in part a reaction to these reports that
led to the publication of *Kritik des Herzens* (Critique of the Heart),
a collection of eighty poems without pictures. For *Dideldum,* Bassermann had been able to convince the author that drawings would
enhance the appeal of his verse. This time Busch claimed that he
had to demonstrate his ability to ride Pegasus unaided. Even if this
was not his real motivation, his defensive posture is significant. He
was probably aware of the risk involved in leaving the relatively
safe area of objectively depicting "outline beings" for the realm of
contemplative poetry. Here the danger of misinterpretation was
increased by the audience's frequent failure to distinguish between
poet and persona. Yet the conviction that he had something valuable
to share, and the desire to be recognized as more than an amusing
entertainer made him willing to incur that risk.

As a child, Busch had read Kant's *Kritik der reinen Vernunft*
(*Critique of Pure Reason*) which, "although only imperfectly un-
derstood at that time," had stimulated his desire to "catch mice in
the chamber of the brain where, however, there are just too many
holes" (4.208). The title he chose was clearly meant to evoke the
association with the philosopher's three major works. It also repeats the deliberate ambiguity of Kant's title: *Kritik* is "criticism"
or "critique." Kant, aware of the original meaning of the word,
interpreted "critique" as "judgment." Moreover, the genitive case
adds to the ambiguity. Do the poems represent judgment origina-

99

ting from the heart rather than the intellect? Or do they judge the
human heart itself? A close reading reveals that both meanings are
intended. But the shift from Kant's "reason" to "that red thing in
my chest" that "sometimes throbs with pain and sometimes with
joy" (2.495), as Busch called it with characteristic understatement,
marks a definite rejection of the philosopher's rationalism. Indeed,
Schopenhauer's impact is more noticeable in the book than Kant's.
"Critique of the Heart" sounds like a Romantic response to the age
of Enlightenment. In fact some of the poetry included in the
volume is Romantic in tone and feeling. But the heart is also the
target, and frequently Busch emerges as a Realist, satirizing and
castigating the fashionable neo-Romanticism of Geibel, Heyse, and
their followers.

When the volume appeared in 1874, the ambiguity of the poems
must have been especially confusing to an audience that had a
preconceived idea of Busch's work. Actually, many of the
techniques used in the texts for the picture stories do occur again,
and some of the witty poems deal with topics treated earlier:
marital problems, children's views of the world, religious hypocrisy, enjoyment of wine or other pleasures of life, and the rude
destruction of beautiful illusions. But without the funny pictures
Busch's statements were harder to accept. More clearly than before did he challenge traditional concepts by unmasking charity
and pity as love of self—as Nietzsche did at approximately the same
time—by revealing hypocrisy and ambition as the compelling
forces in his society, and by pleading for a healthier attitude
toward the relation between the sexes. Some poems are autobiographical, others were misinterpreted as personal confessions because the readers were unable to recognize the ironic intentions.
Sometimes the tone is lyrical and tender, even sentimental. Frequently, however, there is an alienating and sobering conclusion to
such pieces, again very much in the style of Heinrich Heine,
whose *Buch der Lieder* (*Book of Songs*) provided the most direct
model for the arrangement of the book. Like Heine, Busch affixes
no titles to his short poems. The use of colloquialisms and foreign
words can also be found in the earlier poet. But these parallels did
little to win an audience that was not yet ready to accept Heine as
a true representative of German literature.

The first poem in the collection rejects any pretentiousness and
tries to set the tone for the pieces to follow:

Es wohnen die hohen Gedanken
In einem hohen Haus.
Ich klopfte, doch immer hieß es:
Die Herrschaft fuhr eben aus!

Nun klopf ich ganz bescheiden
Bei kleineren Leuten an.
Ein Stückel Brot, ein Groschen
Ernähren auch ihren Mann.

(Lofty thoughts reside / In a lofty home. / I knocked, but was told every time:/ Master and Mistress just went out for a ride!// Now I very modestly knock / On simpler people's doors. / A slice of bread, a penny / Are enough to subsist on.) (2.494)

The second poem, in a light vein, encourages the reader to praise freely in order to be praised himself. But, sensing a negative reaction, the author concludes with an ironic description of the sentiments of the faultfinder who can "hover with great pleasure, elevated above everybody" (2.494). Then follows the well-known account of the bird who sings cheerfully in the face of certain doom and who thus exemplifies humor. A brief curriculum vitae comes next, emphasizing the rhythmic alternation of hope and disappointment of one who "wanted to be something proper," but found that usually things did not work out. Regardless of where he might turn, that "red thing" in his chest will continue to press him on (2.495). The fifth poem is obviously meant for critics objecting to the brevity of most pieces in the collection. Wittily, Busch made the porter of the Weidenbusch Hotel in Frankfort his spokesman, "a poet, but always brief, because he could not think of much." He blames the hectic pace of contemporary life for the laconic tendency. Even Schiller, were he to come back, would no longer be so long-winded in this era of telegrams. The next piece praises the advantages of self-criticism: if you find fault with yourself, you appear very modest; people will be impressed with your honesty; you foil other critics by taking the initiative; and you can expect immediate disagreement on the part of those who want to defend you against yourself—thus you finally emerge as an outstanding character.

These six brief poems, seen as a whole, serve as a valuable introduction to the entire collection. Busch stressed his intention not to imitate the "lofty" tone of classical literature, and to aim for a general audience, not a snobbish elite. His humorous approach and down-to-earth language, on the other hand, did not attempt to disguise the underlying seriousness. His view of human character with all its weaknesses is critical, and the presentation of his findings is tinged with irony, but he does not set himself up as a judge. He is willing to take an unflattering look at himself, too, and to share some of his private feelings and experiences in only slightly generalized form with his readers. His wit and humor—like the chirping of the doomed bird—have to be seen against the backdrop of constant defeat and disillusionment, and the philosophy expressed is essentially pessimistic. But the "red thing" will continue to throb with pain and joy, and the bird will continue to sing until eaten by the black cat: Schopenhauer's "will" manifests itself repeatedly. The human heart is being judged, but the judgment is not based on cold reason; it comes from the heart as well.

The image of the human animal in *Kritik des Herzens* attests to Busch's astute power of observation and his insight into psychological realities. The introductory poems had already established the theme of vanity as a motivating force. Throughout the book, there are further variations of this idea. The fable of the haughty sack of grain can easily be interpreted as reflecting the attitude of self-satisfied human beings who do not realize that they too would be empty shells were it not for others giving them substance. The man who spends a long time in front of the mirror before saying farewell to his "beloved image," and then gets annoyed at the vanity of other people is surely a common type. But those laughing at this caricature were probably stunned by the psychological perception of the arrogant beggar who refuses to show gratitude for a generous gift since he knows that the giver feels sufficiently rewarded by his own vanity.

Busch analyzed the complex emotions that result from observing the bad luck of others: you feel sorry for the person who has met with misfortune because you can see yourself in his place. The realization that you were lucky gives the situation a certain appeal: "Du merkst, daß die Bedaurerei / So eine Art von Wonne sei" ("You realize that feeling sorry / Is some sort of pleasure") (2.520). It is only a short step from this sensation of enjoying pity to pure, undisguised *Schadenfreude,* as exemplified in the poem about the proud rider whom everybody watches with pleasure. He provides increased happiness, however, when his horse throws him. Bassermann urged his author to replace this poem and one on "Uncle Kaspar's red nose" with "something sentimental" (2.554). Busch paid no attention to the request.

In the interest of getting along with one another, people rarely reveal their true feelings. After painting a gloomy picture of what would happen if we always told the truth, Busch praises courtesy, "that delicate deception": "You understand; I understand; and everybody is pleased" (2.506). Schopenhauer, in his *Essays*, had called courtesy "a tacit agreement to ignore mutually each other's miserable moral and intellectual condition and not to disclose it before each other—whereby this condition, to the advantage of both parties, comes to light a little less easily."[1] Another poem describes how the speaker has learned from bitter experience and now cheerfully tells lies when asked direct questions.

The moral code of a society in which deception and hypocrisy are common is examined further. Along with *Schadenfreude,* there is also the envy of those who are more fortunate, especially if we feel that they are less deserving than we are. The poem dealing with this attitude starts out with heavy irony: "Mein kleinster Fehler ist der Neid" ("Envy is my smallest vice") (2.519). As in the lecture on morality that Helena received from her relatives, virtue is seen as a function of one's age and station in life. People tend to be very moral when they are no longer capable of indulging in the pleasures of life. The bird who once enjoyed picking other people's berries wherever he found them has settled down now, taken a wife, and is preaching virtuous conduct to others. As soon as he has his own cherry tree, he curses the sparrows (2.504).

The bourgeois ideal of the *Gründerjahre* is perhaps best exemplified by the devastating portrayal of the pillar of society who considers himself to be absolutely indispensable. He is always active, always involved, always present, whether at dances, horse races, as a judge in competitions, or testing fire engines:

> Ohne ihn war nichts zu machen,
> Keine Stunde hatt' er frei.
> Gestern, als sie ihn begruben,
> War er richtig auch dabei.

(Without him, nothing could be done, / He never had a free hour. / Yesterday, when they buried him, / He was properly present, too.) (2.502)

Another poem warns that society's judgment may not be final: an "old book" tells about a young man who had led a life of passion, who had wasted his property, had been driven by desire, and had committed many sins in his urge to savor everything his existence could offer. A violent accident brings sudden death. "I hope, however—the chronicler says at this point—that grace will lend its pinions to the youth." But the same old book also reports about an honest, worthy, churchgoing citizen who is highly respected in his community. The chronicler comments: "I am only afraid that the philistine will not sprout wings" (2.510–11). Although Busch was on solid Biblical ground here, it is easy to see why the average reader would resent such ideas.

A certain Gustav Spiess from Leipzig probably spoke for many when he described his reaction to *Kritik des Herzens* as one of "revulsion and disgust" and called the collection a "trivial, insipid, and obscene mass" (2.555). The charge of "obscenity" obviously referred to Busch's frank discussion of questions of love and sex. The repressed sexuality of the elderly spinster Miss Schmöle shows in her efforts to keep her maid from enjoying her youth. In her concern for Rieke's salvation, she listens late at night at the girl's bedroom door to make sure that she is in and is resting peacefully, and that nobody is doing anything to her that is "godless and enviable" (2.503). Similarly, the three aunts seem to be motivated by envy of youth when they discuss a present for their niece. They decide on a dress the girl is certain not to like. That way, she will get very angry and still must thank them for it (2.507).

There are a number of rather conventional love songs that would not be out of place in a collection of Romantic verse. In the context of this book, they appear as a deliberate counterbalance to the satire on the relationship between the sexes as it is presented in many of the satirical pieces. The desire of lovers to become one, like a brook and a stream, and to flow "united in sweet waves" toward the ocean, probably seemed absurd to the burgher of the Bismarck era (2.519). The power of love is effectively demonstrated by a short poem that Schopenhauer could have used as an illustrative example for his discussion of the metaphysics of sexual love:

> Ferne Berge seh ich glühen!
> Unruhvoller Wandersinn!
> Morgen will ich weiterziehen,
> Weiß der Teufel, wohin?
>
> Ja ich will mich nur bereiten,
> Will—was hält mich nur zurück?

> Nichts wie dumme Kleinigkeiten!
> Zum Exempel, Dein Blick!

(I see distant mountains glow! / Restless urge to roam! / Tomorrow I will travel on, / Devil knows, whereto? // Yes, I will get ready, / I will—what is holding me back? / Only silly trifles! / As, for example, your glance!) (2.504)

In a letter announcing the book to Johanna Kessler, Busch mentioned that she would recognize "a few familiar sounds" in it (B, 1.126). Perhaps this poem was one of those sounds. And personal experience—possibly the unsuccessful courtship of Anna Richter in 1864—may have inspired the poem about the pretty flower that was cherished by a young butterfly. But then the horrified lover has to witness the end of the object of his adoration: "An old donkey ate the entire / Plant that he had loved so ardently" (2.522).

A charming childhood scene is sketched when the speaker recalls the pretty young lady in her low-cut green dress who used to sit across the dinner table from him. Not given to excessive piety—as is typical of children—the little boy would often think, as grace was being said: "How beautiful Mary looks!" (2.509). The child's natural and healthy attitude toward sex is effectively contrasted with the reactions of an adult society that "cloaks in guilty darkness" what is claimed to be "of all our deeds the most beautiful activity" (2.510).

The theme of marriage is dealt with repeatedly. Two young people ready to become husband and wife, even though neither has any worldly goods, are warned not to "start a war without having the necessary means" (2.515). Perhaps even more devastating than this reference to marriage as the battle of the sexes is the cool description of the couple whose love had once been passionate, but who have now succumbed to a life of routine and comfort:

> Bei eines Strumpfes Bereitung
> Sitzt sie im Morgenhabit;
> Er liest in der Kölnischen Zeitung
> Und teilt ihr das Nötige mit.

(Engaged in the production of a stocking, / She is sitting there in her dressing gown; / He is reading the Cologne News / And communicates to her whatever is necessary.) (2.512)

Readers of today are often struck by the very modern tone, and the

comparison with a poem like Erich Kästner's "Sachliche Romanze"
(Prosaical Romance) has frequently been made.

Throughout the collection, there are traces of Busch's continuing
occupation with Schopenhauer. Whenever man seems to be happy
with his world, or convinced that he is in control of his life, a sudden
ache in his tooth or toe painfully demonstrates to him that he had
been under an illusion: "Pain is the master, and joy is the slave"
(2.522). It is also quite in line with Schopenhauer's view that sexual
attraction can interfere with man's striving for self-control. Love
reduces a highly intelligent male, who had no use for laughter and
joking, to "the greatest fool at the court of the queen of his heart"
(2.517). The belief in the continued existence of the will, independent of the individual's life span, leads to the idea that if we were to be
drowned in a new deluge—as we deserve—we would crawl out of the
mud again and remain essentially unchanged (2.502).

But, as he had shown before, Busch could not go along with
Schopenhauer's suggested voluntary negation of the will. He tells a
self-proclaimed "ascetic" that if he truly were what he pretends to be,
"Crack! with a single jerk you would bring the course of the world to a
halt" (2.522). This philosophical poem is the first of the six pieces that
conclude the collection, and again Busch's careful arrangement is
evident. The lighthearted tone of much of the preceding verse is
gone, and a more contemplative mood prevails, designed to leave the
reader thoughtful and serious. Instead of witticisms, there is nostalgia
and melancholy, especially in the poem whose very first line recalls
Romantic longing: "Du hast das schöne Paradies verlassen" ("You left
the beautiful paradise behind"). Lured on by pleasant and promising
specters, you vaguely feel that every step separates you further from
home. But you have torn the connecting thread, and suddenly you
realize that there is no return:

> Vergebens steht ob deinem Haupt der Stern.
> Einsam, gefangen, von der Heimat fern,
> Ein Sklave, starrst du in des Stromes Lauf
> Und hängst an Weiden deine Harfe auf.
>
> 'Nun fährst du wohl empor, wenn so zuzeiten
> Im stillen Mondlicht durch die Saiten
> Ein leises, wehmutsvolles Klagen geht
> Von einem Hauch, der aus der Heimat weht.

(In vain the star shines high above your head. / Alone, inprisoned, far from home, / A slave, you stare into the river's flow / And hang your harp upon the willows. // You do start up, when at times / A soft, plaintive moaning rings / Over the chords in the moonlight, / From a gentle breeze that comes from home.) (2.523)

The vocabulary and the images are reminiscent of Eichendorff's lyrical verse, and one can even find direct parallels. But, as Marxer points out, the Romantic poet wrote in the assurance that he could still return home, that his soul could spread its wings and fly through the quiet moonlight back to the paradise left behind. Busch's protagonist, however, is denied such flight. His harp is hanging on a tree—it is not the poet who creates his song but the wind that is playing with the instrument.[2]

The next short poem tries to console the melancholy reader, encouraging him to love, sing, and drink, despite the transitoriness of time, and to remember: "Even a gentle wink of the eye flashes through all eternity" (2.523). It is only fitting that this last statement is followed immediately by the poem elegizing Busch's sister Anna who had died in 1858 at the age of fifteen:

> Nun, da die Frühlingsblumen wieder blühen,
> In milder Luft die weißen Wolken ziehen,
> Denk ich mit Wehmut deiner Lieb und Güte,
> Du süßes Mädchen, das so früh verblühte.

(Now that spring flowers bloom again, / White clouds drift in the gentle air, / I think of your love and kind heart with sadness, / You sweet girl who had to wither away so soon.)

After recollecting her life and death, the writer concluded: "Wo du auch seist; im Herzen bleibst du mein. / Was Gutes in mir lebt, dein ist's allein" ("Wherever you may be, in my heart you will remain mine. / Whatever good is alive in me is yours alone") (2.524).

Bassermann confessed that this poem had moved him more than any verse he had read in a long time. Even Gustav Spiess must have liked it. He referred to the two poems "dedicated to a deceased sweetheart" which "reveal indeed a delicate poetic talent" (2.555). The other piece he had in mind was probably the last poem in the book, an epitaph for the poet's mother. But these two very personal accounts are separated by a "fairy tale, pretty and profound." This sequence is very skillful: some relief is provided from what might have become overwhelmingly melancholy or sentimental. But the nostalgic mood and essentially Romantic flavor remain undisturbed. Busch utilized the folkloristic motif of man's soul leaving his body temporarily in the form of a mouse. While the shepherd boy is sleeping, a little white mouse jumps from his mouth and runs into an old horse's skull bleached by sun and rain. While investigating the cavities of the skull, the mouse is startled by the sudden mooing of a cow nearby, and quickly returns to where it had come from. The awakening boy tells of his beautiful dream in which he had entered a castle of white marble and met a lovely princess who offered him her heart and wealth. At that moment there was a sudden and loud blast of a trumpet, and princess, castle, and everything disappeared.

Busch's mother had died in 1870. The poem addressed to her attests not only to his strong emotional attachment but, in its intricate metric scheme, also to his poetic ambition and to the debt he owed to the Romantic movement where similar experimentation was common:

> O du, die mir die Liebste war,
> Du schläfst nun schon so manches Jahr.
> So manches Jahr, da ich allein,
> Du gutes Herz, gedenk ich dein.
> Gedenk ich dein, von Nacht umhüllt,
> So tritt zu mir dein treues Bild.
> Dein treues Bild, was ich auch tu,
> Es winkt mir ab, es winkt mir zu.
> Und scheint mein Wort dir gar zu kühn,
> Nicht gut mein Tun,
> Du hast mir einst so oft verziehn,
> Verzeih auch nun.

(You, whom I have loved most of all, / You have been sleeping now for many a year. / For many a year I have been alone, / Oh loving heart, when I have been thinking of you. / When I have been thinking of you, enwrapped by night, / To me appeared your faithful image. / Your faithful image, whatever I do, / It gestures warning, it gestures encouragement. / And if my word seems all too bold to you, / My actions not right, / You have forgiven me so often, / Forgive this time, too.) (2. 526)

But the general audience was not willing to forgive Busch's bold words and uncomfortable insights. One of the few readers who showed appreciation was Maria Anderson. Her enthusiastic letter of praise was especially welcome in the face of widespread negative reactions or lack of interest. It was to be almost thirty years before his second volume of poetry was to appear.

II   In the End (1904)

In February 1904, Busch asked Bassermann whether he would be interested in printing another collection of verse. The author indicated that his "life's little thread" was "becoming increasingly thinner and shorter" (B, 2.219). Three days later he mailed the manuscript of one hundred poems to be published in the same format as the earlier volume. In April, *Zu guter Letzt* (In the End), the last of his works to appear during his lifetime, was already available to the public.

Busch's sense of urgency is evident. At seventy-two, he had to consider each additional day granted him as a special gift. His awareness of living on borrowed time was painfully increased by the news of the impending death of his close friend Lenbach, four years his junior. Significantly, Busch suggested the publication of his poems in the same letter that acknowledged the sad tidings. He saw this book as his last message. Its title indicates finality as well as the attempt to epitomize the insights of a life of keen observation. "Zu guter Letzt" can also be translated as "to sum up." The request to duplicate the format of the collection published a generation earlier indicates a desire for continuity. In the interest of this consistency, Busch omitted the original titles for the individual poems which were restored in posthumous editions. As before, he did not arrange the poems chronologically but aimed for effective grouping and delicate balancing. The introductory and concluding pieces are therefore again of special importance.

The opening poem, "Beschränkt" (Limited), is indicative of the tolerance and resignation that grew out of seven decades of looking at human ambitions and failures:

> Halt dein Rößlein nur im Zügel,
> Kommst ja doch nicht allzuweit.
> Hinter jedem neuen Hügel
> Dehnt sich die Unendlichkeit.
> Nenne niemand dumm und säumig,
> Der das Nächste recht bedenkt.

Ach, die Welt ist so geräumig,
Und der Kopf ist so beschränkt.

(Just rein your little horse, / You won't get very far anyway. / Behind each new
hill / There stretches infinity. / Don't call anybody stupid or tardy / Who is
giving much thought to the next step. / Oh, the world is so spacious, / And
one's head is so limited.) (4.265)

The theme of tolerance recurs in the next piece, "Geschmackssache"
(Matter of Taste), which has the same function of preparing the reader
for what is to come as the poem about "a slice of bread, a penny" in the
earlier volume: tables are set with different food for different people,
and one should allow anybody his enjoyment as long as he sticks to his
own plate. But if someone impudently bothers you at your own table,
"then just give him a smack so that he'll learn what is proper" (4.266).
The mood then becomes more philosophical in "Durchweg leben-
dig" (Alive Throughout) which gives evidence of Busch's interest in
science, and of his insight into the essence of matter. For him,
nothing is dead, and "force is alive everywhere." Even a firm rock is
"a cooperative of forces." Singularities, striving to be this way or that,
make up this variegated world (4.266).
As if to defend himself against the charge of presenting a basically
materialistic world view in "Alive Throughout," Busch followed
immediately with a folkloristic tale about the ferryman who is asked to
take some passengers over the Rhine. He cannot see anybody in the
moonlight, but his boat is loaded heavily, and on the other side of the
river, each of the ghostly travelers throws a gold coin into the ferry.
The last two lines show that this narrative was meant as a philosophical statement. The ferryman muses: "Such souls are invisible, to be
sure, and yet there is something to it" (4.267).
The idea of continued existence after death is approached from a
different angle in the next piece. "Nachruhm" (Posthumous Fame)
reminds us that an artist lives on in his works. But, as so often, the
lofty thought is expressed in ironic language: our mouths will continue to mention the poet in rapture for a long time, so that "he'll
live in great happiness between our hollow teeth" (4.267). The irony
is in part directed at the author himself. The astute reader could see
the connection with the following poem, "Der alte Narr" (The Old
Fool), about the aging tightrope walker ready to retire. His disappointed audience talks about his being too weak and too stiff to climb

up again, so he feels honor-bound to demonstrate once more that he has not lost his ability. As can be expected, he falls. The old fool will never walk straight again, as the witnesses of the accident state without a trace of sympathy.

A comparison of this group of poems with the six pieces that set the tone for *Kritik des Herzens* reveals both the similarities and the differences between the two books. At first glance, the parallels are striking. The same "unpoetic" language, the same tendency toward ironic understatement and disillusionment, the same critical look at the ways of mankind, but again tempered with humor: it appears that Busch suggested the same format for the two books because he saw their essential similarity. But a closer look reveals important differences in tone, emphasis, and outlook. The self-conscious and somewhat defensive posture of turning away from "lofty thoughts" in their "lofty house" has given way to the wise recognition of human limitations in general. While there is still a willingness to rebuff anybody who infringes upon the private sphere, there is also greater tolerance. The belief in the perpetuity of life is evident—whether in the form of active and "lively" matter, in the traditional view of man's immortal soul, or through creative works that will live on. The comparatively greater emphasis on death and afterlife, and the more introspective mood mark *Zu guter Letzt* as a late work. It is quite fitting that one of the poems in the introductory group is based on folk tradition. The motifs from fairy tales and legends seem to be more numerous in this collection. The aging writer returned to the world of his youth.

Several poems in the book are based on Busch's "Spricker" ("sprigs"), a collection of aphorisms and poetic notes discovered in his estate and named after a short verse found among them. Frequently he would cross out an item after having utilized it for a poem. In some instances, the transition from a short but often strikingly formulated idea—reminiscent of Lichtenberg's brilliant notes—to an elaborate poetic structure offers insights into Busch's literary procedure. Occasionally the concise statement of the "Spricker" seems more effective than the longer version: " 'God's reward!' said the beggar, and then the loaf of bread slipped through his basket" (4.547) has the brevity and flavor of a popular proverb. The beggar in "Unberufen" (Knock on Wood!) hobbles through the village on crutches, his old basket on his shoulders. He knocks on every door in vain. At the very last house he finds a good woman who has just buried her third

husband and consequently is in a mood for charity. She puts a
seven-pound loaf of bread into his basket, and he happily praises his
good fortune as he crosses a wild stream on a little bridge. That is the
moment when the bread slips through the defective container. A final
line summarizes the moral: "That's what you get for being so
presumptuous" (4.269). The clarity of the intended statement is
diminished in this case by the more elaborate account. The reader
develops a sympathetic mood that interferes with the appreciation of
the concluding line. Furthermore, the explanation for the charitable
action by the widow is irrelevant to the main idea and focuses
attention on her rather than on the unfortunate hero of the tale.
Often, however, Busch developed the aphorisms into significant
poetic versions.

One of the "sprigs" reads: "The sinner—thus everybody—should
at least possess self-irony" (4.544). While self-irony was characteristic
of much of Busch's literary production, it seems even more prevalent
in this volume. "Erneuerung" (Renovation) tells of the economical
mother who fashions a new jacket for her son from his father's old
tailcoat:

> Grad so behilft sich der Poet.
> Du liebe Zeit, was soll er machen?
> Gebraucht sind die Gedankensachen
> Schon alle, seit die Welt besteht.

(The poet makes do in exactly the same way. / Good heavens, what is he
supposed to do?/ All of that thought stuff has been used/ Since the world
came into being.) (4.307)

Johannes Klein misses the self-irony in this perhaps overly modest
concept of poetic creation when he assumes that Busch's targets in
this poem were incompetent would-be poets like Baldwin Baalamb,
and that therefore the comparison between literary production and
mending clothes was on the same level as the milk-and-butter
metaphor in the picture story of the "poet manqué."[3]

Equally ironic is the view of unmarried life in "Der Einsame" (The
Lonely One), a paraphrase of a Jung-München piece. Wilhelm
Busch, the lifelong bachelor, praised the happy existence of one who
is not bothered by animal, man, or piano, who does not have to listen
to good advice, who can dress and behave in his own home as he
pleases, who is allowed to mend his own clothing, who is forgotten by

the world and will not be missed after his demise. The first and last lines are identical: "He who is lonely is well off" (4.324–25).

In "Beiderseits" (Mutual), the aging poet parodies a poem by Walther von der Vogelweide. In a letter to Marie Hesse, Busch quoted from the elegy of the medieval bard, "Owê war sint verswunden alliu mîniu jâr!" ("Alas, where have all my years gone!"), when he wrote: "I have received more than my quota of years. As long as I am feeling reasonably well, I will gratefully accept the bonus, even though I often ask myself with Walther von der Vogelweide: Has my life been a dream, or is it real?" (B, 2.246). Another of Walther's late poems presents a dialogue in which the poet bids farewell to "Frô Welt" ("Lady World") and her house whose host is the devil. She tries to persuade him to stay, but he has finally realized the fleetingness of worldly beauty and the insignificance of human possessions, and he leaves for a more permanent resting place.[4] Busch's short poem adds an ironic twist to the medieval verse. When his "Sir Walter" tells Lady World that she is getting grey and wrinkled, and that her figure is sad to behold, the pert response is: "Dear Sir, you should rather be quiet! You yourself do not seem to be as handsome anymore with your black spectacles" (4.298).

Many of the poems deal with nature. The idea of "Alive Throughout" is formulated even more strikingly in "Die Kleinsten" (The Smallest Ones), which sounds almost prophetic:

> Sag Atome, sage Stäubchen.
> Sind sie auch unendlich klein,
> Haben sie doch ihre Leibchen
> Und die Neigung da zu sein.
>
> Haben sie auch keine Köpfchen,
> Sind sie doch voll Eigensinn.
> Trotzig spricht das Zwerggeschöpfchen:
> Ich will sein so wie ich bin.
>
> Suche sie nur zu bezwingen,
> Stark und findig wie du bist.
> Solch ein Ding hat seine Schwingen,
> Seine Kraft und seine List.
>
> Kannst du auch aus ihnen schmieden
> Deine Rüstung als Despot,

Schließlich wirst du doch ermüden,
Und dann heißt es: Er ist tot.

(Call them atoms, call them dust specks. / Infinitely small as they are, / They nevertheless have their bodies / And their inclination to exist. // Even though they don't have heads, / They are still very stubborn. / Obstinately, the tiny being states:/ I want to be as I am. // Much as you try to conquer them,/ Strong and clever as you are,/ Such an object has wings of its own,/ Has energy and has cunning. // Even if you can forge from them / Your armor as a despot, / Eventually you will grow weary, / And then it will be said: He died.) (4.317)

After Hiroshima and Nagasaki, few would agree with Eduard Engel's assessment of the volume containing this poem as "peculiar," "rustically quiet," and "grandfatherly" (4.555).

Busch carefully studied the small world around him. Whether he describes the attitude of impertinent sparrows or the damage done by hungry titmice; whether the animals observed are caterpillars in the cabbage patch, snails in the garden, or plant lice on the roses; whether the life cycle of mosquitoes is sketched or the biography of a mole: each of the miniatures, often reminiscent of the close-ups of plants and small animals in the nature poetry of Annette von Droste-Hülshoff, places Busch in the tradition of Poetic Realism. Like many of the works of Meyer, Storm, and Keller, these poems are based on personal observation and experience, but also serve as vehicles for the author's philosophy. "Hund und Katze" (Dog and Cat) can serve as an example. After visiting Bachmann at Ebergötzen in March 1899, Busch told Grete Meyer of his friend's little dog Molly who served as the wet nurse and adoptive mother for five little cats, three grey ones and two black ones (B, 2.143). In the poetic version, he uses the actual name of the dog. He tells about the enmity between her and Miezel, the cat, which lasts until the latter is killed by the game warden. After a brief report of Molly's adoption of the five orphans, the poem concludes with a statement that reveals a more positive view of the world than could be found in many of his earlier works:

Mensch mit traurigem Gesichte,
Sprich nicht nur von Leid und Streit.
Selbst in Brehms Naturgeschichte
Findet sich Barmherzigkeit.

(Oh man, with the sad look on your face, / Don't talk just about suffering and strife. / Even in Brehm's work on natural history, / It is possible to find charity.) (4.312)

Characteristically, however, this heartwarming story was followed by a poem about the shy man who, after a long time of vacillation, finally proposes to his beloved in writing. When she politely declines, the shock over the unexpected response affects him "as if a rat had suddenly bitten his heart"(4.312). A similarly ineffective lover is ridiculed in "Scheu und treu" (Bashful and Faithful). The young man adores his lady from a distance. His moment of greatest bliss comes when one of her blond and curly hairs falls into his soup. He will always carry it in a locket right over the spot "where his faithful heart is beating" (4.281). As Johannes Klein states, a poem like Schiller's "Ritter Toggenburg," romanticizing this type of impotent love, was no longer possible after such devastating portrayal.[5]

As in *Kritik des Herzens,* numerous poems show Busch's understanding of human psychology or offer advice, some of it serious, some in an ironic vein. "Kopf und Herz" (Head and Heart) observes how people react much more violently if their intelligence is questioned than if doubts are raised about their ethical standards. The dubious moral position of Miss Schmöle is stated again in more generalized form in "Die Schändliche" (The Scandalous Woman). A charming young woman is described who is enjoying a life unfettered by moral conventions. The "morally superior people" can only "complain happily about this disgraceful person" and "painfully envy her" (4.270).

One of Busch's aphorisms reads: "People love cheese, but they cover it. Vice" (4.546). This line—without the explanatory last word—serves as the conclusion of a short piece, "Pst!" (Hush!), which suggests that certain "charming and spicy" topics are not suitable for conversations (4.273). This advice appears quite appropriate from a writer who avoided suggestiveness and erotic innuendo in his work while pleading for more natural attitudes. Other recommendations are facetious, however, and actually constitute barely disguised attacks on society's hypocrisy. Busch, who had always treasured his individuality, suggests in "Wie üblich" (As Usual) that one should not try to be different but rather walk the trodden path. If you are of the same opinion as everybody else, people will meet you with kindness. Many a person who tried to break away from the crowd has lost his way and ended in the underbrush. An even harsher indictment of society is "Strebsam" (Ambitious). The poem encourages anybody who wants to get ahead in the world to keep his thoughts to himself, to bow, to deceive, to flatter, to give up his own views, "because, naturally, only by lying will you get anywhere" (4.284).

Earlier Busch had ridiculed the arrogant rejection of Darwin's teachings by self-satisfied burghers. In "Die Affen" (The Monkeys), he returns to that theme. A boy, after listening to his father's unflattering description of the monkeys in the zoo, concludes that they are actually people. The reference to the animal nature of man ties in with the belief in the primacy of evil rather than good in human character that Busch had often stressed. "Nicht artig" (Not Well-Behaved) makes a summary statement: we are by nature no angels, but rather "children of the world and of man," and all around us there is a crowd of similar beings. Therefore, to assure any order in the world, consideration of others has to be beaten into everybody from the very beginning. This, of course, means that we cannot afford to be ourselves: "Du darfst nicht zeigen, was du bist. / Wie schad, o Mensch, daß dir das Gute / Im Grunde so zuwider ist" ("You may not reveal what you are. / What a pity, oh man, that, basically, / Virtue is so odious to you" (4.286).

Busch shared with Schopenhauer the belief in palingenesis. In his correspondence with Maria Anderson, he saw each birth as a rebirth. Our fear of death is mainly caused by our uncertainty as to the specific form in which we might reappear (B, 1.144, 145, 148). Unlike Schopenhauer, he did not make a distinction between palingenesis and metempsychosis, but saw both as proofs of the continued reemergence of the will. In "Seelenwanderung" (Metempsychosis), he states that it is human nature to want to be reborn if given a chance, regardless of how miserable life might be. Even "an old, blind man" will elect to "return another thousand times" (4.273).

The idea of rebirth is also expressed in "Der Kobold" (The Goblin), based on the aphorism: "Death: Even if the house burns down, the goblin moves along to the other lodgings" (4.543). Busch used a folkloristic motif for his allegory. A mischievous elf harasses the inhabitants of a house whose first floor is "occupied by the stomach." Plagued by the eternal noise, the desperate owner burns down his home and builds a new one elsewhere, but to no avail: the goblin has come along and continues to make life miserable. When the unlucky man finally asks him who he is, the elf responds laughingly: "I am your self" (4.296).

To Busch and Schopenhauer the human intellect seemed a rather ineffective tool. "Oben und unten" (Above and Below) states that it would be desirable for the head to rule the world, but in reality "the stomach and its accomplices" are in control. "Der Knoten" (The Knot) shows the limitations of man's thinking with equal clarity: in our youthful days, when we are not yet given to meditation, we may find comfort in the belief that our thoughts are free. But eventually we become aware of the tough knot in our brain, and finally, with our pride decreasing, we realize: "Es kann doch unsereiner / Nur denken, wie er muß" ("Our kind can, after all, / Only think the way we must") (4.307).

But Busch saw another realm beyond that of rational philosophy. Parting company with Schopenhauer, he suggested religious faith as an alternative to intellectual speculations. In "Glaube" (Faith), he compares religious belief with a strong castle that cannot be conquered by any enemy. He warns, however, of "excursions into the domain of the intellect" because there one has to conform to the laws of that country, and the result can only be inglorious defeat and a quick retreat to the impenetrable castle (4.277). "Höchste Instanz" (The Highest Authority) asserts that nobody questions what he loves. Rational objections to an emotional state are inappropriate and ineffective since the highest authority has already reached a decision. Thus we should not disturb love, and we should not interfere with faith which is, if seen correctly, also pure love (4.304). Schopenhauer had said: "Faith is like love: it cannot be forced."[6]

"Die Welt" (The World) reflects both the belief in palingenesis and a desire to accept happily whatever life presents. A serious philosophical assertion lies behind the lighthearted tone of the piece. One can understand Solomon's unhappiness with the world: the poor man had to endure the constant chattering of a thousand wives. So if somebody has only one wife—as is the custom today—he should not voice the frequent complaint that he is too good for this world. Even the single man should not be dissatisfied but rather remember that he helped construct this world, and that he botched the job. This realization ought to lead to the cheerful thought: "Gottlob, ich bin kein Salomo;/ Die Welt, obgleich sie wunderlich,/ Ist mehr als gut genug für mich" ("Thank goodness, I am no Solomon;/ This world, even though it is peculiar,/ Is more than good enough for me") (4.293).

Busch's more conciliatory mood can also be seen in the revision of an earlier poem. About 1880, he had written a short fable, "Fink und

Frosch" (The Finch and the Frog), castigating unlimited ambition not coupled with the appropriate skill. The finch is singing a beautiful song from the top of a tree. With great effort, a frog has climbed to the same spot and is adding his voice to that of the bird. When the finch flies off, the frog tries to follow but falls on the hard ground, is "flattened like a cake," and will never croak again. The moral:

> Wenn einer, der mit Mühe kaum
> Geklettert ist auf einen Baum,
> Schon meint, daß er ein Vogel wär,
> So irrt sich der.

(If someone, who, with great effort, / Has barely managed to climb up a tree, / Already imagines himself a bird / Then he is mistaken.) (4.515)

The new version retains the title, the plot, and the message. But the ambitious frog luckily lands on his soft and fat belly and is unhurt. The poem ends with ironic praise for the animal's unwillingness to accept nature's limitations: "Hail to him! He carried it out" (4.279).

The tone of *Zu guter Letzt* is not uniform. The Realist who would regale his readers with a detailed poetic description of the preparation of pancakes and salad—an obvious counterpart to his praise of a juicy roast in *Kritik des Herzens*—was also capable of evoking a completely different mood. In one of his most personal poems, whose very title, "Sehnsucht" (Longing), betrays again his indebtedness to the Romantic movement, Busch voiced his sadness at an existence based on doing evil. Man causes killing in order to live. This recognition creates anxiety because the plaintive voice has never been stilled that urges in the depth of one's heart: "Be good again." Deep within, the poet senses the vague longing for a better world that existed long ago. He yearns for a return of the "first happiness," the "peace of paradise of old, when no lamb yet shunned the wolf" (4.273). But modern man can find such peace only in his dreams.

A dream vision starts the concluding triad of poems, just as the shepherd's dream had formed part of the lyrical finale of the earlier volume. "Der Traum" (The Dream) is a concise verse counterpart to Edward's nocturnal travels and to Peter's odyssey in Busch's two prose tales. The narrator relates how, in his dream, his self had left his body and arrived in a beautiful region, the realm of the butterflies. A lovely woman joined the dreamer but disappeared just when he had made up his mind to embrace her and to hold on to her forever. It was becoming very warm; a cool brook promised refreshment. As he bowed down to the water, a cold, pale arm reached out from the bottom to pull him in. He struggled free, but his neck remained crooked and stiff for good. With some pain and difficulty, he looked around and saw that everything had turned sad and empty. All the butterflies were gone, and the flowers which were in bloom a moment ago had withered. As he was limping on, a witch suddenly jumped on his shoulders, weighing him down and spurring him on until, in total exhaustion, he reached a dark forest. The gaunt figure of a hunter appeared and ordered the weary traveler to stop. An arrow was aimed at his heart, but just before the fatal shot, the dream abruptly ended (4.329–30). This vision might outline a journey through life, from the butterfly world of youth through a frustrated love encounter to the stage of old age when the years become heavier and heavier loads to carry until there is the final confrontation with the hunter whose arrow never misses. But even the crippled and exhausted man dreads this moment and will try to "return another thousand times."

This theme of eternal rebirth is then taken up in "Immer wieder" (Again and Again), in which the cycle of the seasons becomes a symbol for nature's constant renewal. After the fear of death as expressed in the preceding piece, the message here is reassuring, and the colloquial tone effectively contrasts with the Romantic mood of "The Dream." The arrival of summer brings once more "the ever popular wonder stuff" of flowers and of songs. This happens year after year: "What lived, has died; what is, it was; and today becomes tomorrow." Nature is a sculptress who must "always use the old clay for her new designs" (4.331).

The concluding poem shows Busch, at the end of a long and productive life, looking back as well as ahead. The title "Auf Wiedersehn" is meant literally as "until I see you again," not simply as "farewell." A comparison with the original "sprig" is particularly instructive: "Curriculum vitae: Journey; from where, whereto; barking dogs in the village, the small ones do the biting. Lodging and leave-taking (like blind people, until we see each other again). Home and rest" (4.543). The poetic version leaves the interpretation of the "journey" as a metaphor to the reader. The philosophical questions about origin and goals of life have been dropped along with the social commentary about the village dogs. The farewell of the blind comes at the very end, and the poem thus concludes with an expression of hope for a better world where present imperfections no longer exist. The emphasis is not on the journey through life, but on death. Death, however, will lead to new life. The aging poet was firm in his belief, and as he once wrote, "Nur was wir glauben wissen wir gewiß" ("Only what we believe do we know for sure") (B, 1.215). This was Busch's final message to his audience, written in the simple language of a folk song:

Ich schnürte meinen Ranzen
Und kam zu einer Stadt,
Allwo es wir im ganzen
Recht gut gefallen hat.

Nur eines macht beklommen,
So freundlich sonst der Ort:
Wer heute angekommen,
Geht morgen wieder fort.

Bekränzt mit Trauerweiden,
Vorüber zieht der Fluß,
Den jeder beim Verscheiden
Zuletzt passieren muß.

Wohl dem, der ohne Grauen,
In Liebe treu bewährt,
Zu jenen dunklen Auen
Getrost hinüberfährt.

Zwei Blinde, müd vom Wandern,
Sah ich am Ufer stehn,
Der eine sprach zum andern:
Leb wohl, auf Wiedersehn.

(I packed my bags / And arrived in a town / Where, on the whole, / I liked it quite well. // There's only one thing that makes you uneasy, / Friendly as the place is otherwise: / Whoever has arrived today / Will leave again tomorrow. // Adorned with weeping willow trees, / The river is flowing by/ Which everybody, in leaving, / Will have to cross in the end. // Happy he, who without dread, / Proven in faithful love, / In confidence crosses over / To those dark regions. // I saw, standing on the river's bank, / Two blind men, tired of wandering; / Said one to the other: / Farewell, until we see each other again.) (4.331)

III   Appearance and Reality

Schein und Sein (Appearance and Reality) was published posthumously in 1909 by Otto Nöldeke. The book contained poetry found in the author's estate, and the absence of Busch's guidance in selection and arrangement is noticeable. Most of the poems were written between 1899 and 1907 and thus reflect the mood of *Zu guter Letzt*, but some pieces are much older, including even a song from the 1861 libretto for an operetta by Kremplsetzer. A few had been published before in their entirety or in abridged form; other occasional verses, especially lyrical birthday greetings for Nanda Kessler, were never meant for publication. Busch would surely have objected to the inclusion of certain poems, and he would have reworked and polished others before sharing them with the public. Although there are few completely new tones in the volume, the collection is a valuable supplement to the lyrical work published before. Many pieces were probably omitted from *Zu guter Letzt* mainly for reasons of space. As in the earlier book, it is frequently possible to trace poems back to Busch's aphorisms.

Nöldeke took the title for the book from a poem he used as introduction. This choice is fortunate since Busch frequently dealt with the discrepancy between the way things—as well as humans and their actions—look and the way they actually are. Through this opening poem, the reader is also encouraged to go beyond the first impression of the often entertaining verse and look for a more profound message. As Busch pointed out, all the things in this world, whether large or small, are wrapped up in such a way that they cannot simply be cracked like a nut. It is especially difficult to fathom human beings: "You only know them from the outside. / You see their vests and not their hearts" (4.393).

Many of Busch's comments on human character and its shortcomings paraphrase the insights of earlier verse and attest to the consistency of his viewpoint. But there are also a few new themes. In "Rechthaber" (Know-It-All), the reader is warned to avoid the company of the "not very rare phenomenon" of the self-righteous "knight of his own opinion" (4.418). "Modern" deals with the generation conflict: young people are impatient with those "old gentlemen" who refuse to die and leave their estate behind, even though they have ceased to be of use to anybody (4.402). "Niemals" (Never) asserts that nobody is satisfied if he obtains what he had been longing for: "Each wish, once fulfilled, / Immediately gives birth to young ones" (4.406).

Poets and poetry are discussed on several occasions. Masterful in its deliberate ambiguity is "Armer Haushalt" (Poor Household). It could be a description of the economic reality of a poet's existence by a Realist, bent on destroying the Romantic myth of the poor but happy artist. Another interpretation might see a satirical portrait of dilettantes like Baalamb, whose poetic "means" do not match their ambition. The milk-and-butter metaphor that Busch used in the tale of the "prevented poet" lends additional weight to the second view:

> Weh, wer ohne rechte Mittel
> Sich der Poesie vermählt.
> Täglich dünner wird der Kittel,
> Und die Milch im Hause fehlt.
>
> Ängstlich schwitzend muß er sitzen,
> Fort ist seine Seelenruh,
> Und vergeblich an den Zitzen
> Zupft er seine magre Kuh.

(Woe to him who without proper means / Gets wedded to poetry. / His coat wears thinner every day, / And there is a lack of milk in the house. // Sweating anxiously, he has to sit there, / Gone is his peace of mind, / And in vain he is plucking / On the teats of his skinny cow.) (4.409)

"Auch er" (He, Too) deals with the commercial aspects of literary life. Busch had witnessed the lack of success of some of the works that meant most to him. Occasionally, he had taken a strong interest in the promotion of his books. His poem states that a writer can relate "touchingly beautiful tales of the heart," created from his imagination. But he has to make a living. So he goes to the market with his "neatly bound little volumes," everything he has "carefully raked together," in order to sell his ware "just as the farmer does with his little pigs" (4.404). The same self-irony is evident in "Verzeihlich" (Excusable), which starts with the sentence: "He is a poet, therefore vain." But we should not be too harsh on the poet because all he has is the world of beauty and wealth in his "bag of lies." While conjuring up images of castles in the moonlight and beautiful ladies, he is sitting in his unheated room, without money, without a sweetheart, and his feet are getting cold (4.408). If a writer becomes successful, he immediately evokes the envy of everybody. However, as "Befriedigt" (Satisfied) makes clear, if we hear that his marriage broke up, that he is in debt, or that he drinks, our satisfaction returns at once (4.408).

Poets and society had been treated in ironic fashion by Heinrich

Heine, too. But even some of Busch's serious nature lyrics betray his indebtedness to Heine as well as to the Romanticism of Eichendorff. In 1907, Busch had contributed a poem, "Immerhin" (After All), to a volume honoring Adolf Wilbrandt. The four stanzas move from the contemplation of nature to a statement of philosophy. The sunset, the murmuring brooks, the whispering tree induce in the observer a state where immaterial time seems to be vanishing like a dream. He feels that "for ever from the dark depth the lifespring is gushing" (B, 2.267). This actually represented the conclusion of a poem Busch had drafted in 1905. The complete version was now published by Nöldeke, and the first of the two introductory stanzas reads:

> Mein Herz, sei nicht beklommen,
> Noch wird die Welt nicht alt.
> Der Frühling ist wiedergekommen,
> Frisch grünt der deutsche Wald.

(My heart, don't be so anxious, / The world is not yet growing old. / Spring has returned, / The German forest is freshly green.) (4.419).

Perhaps Busch had not included this part in the Wilbrandt volume because he was aware of its similarity with the beginning of a poem in Heine's *Buch der Lieder*:

> Herz, mein Herz, sei nicht beklommen,
> Und ertrage dein Geschick.
> Neuer Frühling gibt zurück,
> Was der Winter dir genommen.[7]

(Heart, my heart, don't be so anxious, / And bear your fate. / A new spring is giving back to you / What winter took away.)

Spring is also celebrated in "Frühlingslied" (Spring Song), a joyful celebration of life that could have been written for Jung-München, but in fact dates from the year before Busch's death. The concluding lines call "to love and to be loved" in May "the most beautiful thing on earth" (4.423). It is on a spring morning that the oneness with all of nature is felt most keenly, as "Vertraut" (Intimate) proclaims. The poet senses "the most beautiful harmony of souls" with all creatures: "We are akin, I feel it deeply, and that is why I love them so" (4.416). The spirit here is more that of Goethe than of Darwin. But Busch never forgot man's destructive role in the harmony of nature. "Bis auf weiteres" (Until Further Notice) describes in a humorous vein the cheerful attitude of people who slaughter and eat pigs "in the manner of cannibals" and will continue to do so until, some day in the future, we will reject the delicious Westphalian ham with utter disgust (4.413). Another example of human interference with nature is a poem which, like that about Molly the dog, was based on a specific experience as described in a letter to Maria Anderson: "The other day, neighbor Mumme was pottering about in his garden with a spade, close to the gooseberry bush. All of a sudden, a strange dog jumps out of there, and snarls, and does not want to leave, and bares its teeth. 'That dog is rabid,' is the immediate verdict. A gun is fetched—bang!—the bullet goes through the head of the dog who stretches and dies.—When people look more closely, there are three very small newborn puppies lying in the bush" (B, 1.143–44). Almost twenty years later this incident grew into a poem, "Der fremde Hund" (The Strange Dog). But the immediacy and freshness of the original prose report are missing, and a more sentimental mood prevails. The last stanza ends with the image of four blind puppies sucking busily on their mother's dead breast (4.402).

The genesis of this poem shows once again how Busch started from direct experience and personal observation in much of his lyrical work. This even holds for some of his contemplative poetry, which is closer to Goethe's philosophical verse than to that of Schiller. Like Goethe, Busch was a "naive" poet by Schiller's definition, since he had not lost the original and intimate tie with nature. There are even echoes of Goethe's language in Busch's poetry. "Gedrungen" (Stocky) can serve as an example:

Schnell wachsende Keime
Welken geschwinde;
Zu lange Bäume
Brechen im Winde.

Schätz nach der Länge
Nicht das Entsprungne;
Fest im Gedränge
Steht das Gedrunge.

(Germs growing fast / Will quickly wither; / Trees too high / Will break in the wind. // Don't judge by height / Whatever arose; / Firmly in the throng / Stands what is stocky.) (4.410)

Of course, Busch's lifelong occupation with Schopenhauer is also reflected in this volume. Joseph Ehrlich asserts that "Woher, wohin?" (Wherefrom, Whereto?) betrays Schopenhauer's impact more than any other of Busch's works.[8] Each statement in the poem can be traced to the views of the Frankfort philosopher, and the pessimism of the last stanza provides an interesting contrast with the affirmative stance of some of the other verse in the book:

> Wo sich Ewigkeiten dehnen,
> Hören die Gedanken auf.
> Nur der Herzen frommes Sehnen
> Ahnt, was ohne Zeitenlauf.
>
> Wo wir waren, wo wir bleiben,
> Sagt kein kluges Menschenwort;
> Doch die Grübelgeister schreiben:
> Bist du weg, so bleibe fort.
>
> Laß dich nicht aufs neu gelüsten.
> Was geschah, es wird geschehn.
> Ewig an des Lebens Küsten
> Wirst du scheiternd untergehn.

(Where eternities are stretching / All thoughts cease. / Only the pious longing of the heart / Senses what is beyond the course of our time. // No wise person's word can tell / Where we were and where we'll remain; / But the ruminating spirits write: / If you're gone, then stay away. // Don't have the same desire anew. / What has happened that will happen. / Forever, on the shores of life, / You will be shipwrecked and go down.) (4.394)

The introductory poem of *Zu guter Letzt* had emphasized the limitations of human understanding, and suggested tolerance and modesty. One of Busch's aphorisms reads: "If you say two times two equals four, that is clear, but empty. If you say sausage, then there is something to it. But who can fathom the essence of a sausage?" (4.542). The poem based on this "sprig," "Beruhigt" (Reassured), repeats the arithmetic "truth" of the aphorism and expresses regret at its shallowness and emptiness. But instead of continuing the discussion of form and content with the example of the sausage, Busch related his search in all directions for the deepest roots of everything and his frequent stumbles in that quest. The aged poet concluded with an idyllic description of the condition after the realization that the intellect is not an adequate tool for finding the ultimate truth:

Endlich baut ich eine Hütte.
Still nun zwischen ihren Wänden
Sitz ich in der Welten Mitte,
Unbekümmert um die Enden.

(Finally I built a hut. / Now I am sitting quietly between its walls / In the middle of the world, / Unconcerned about its ends.) (4.407)

This is the retreat into the castle of faith after the abortive venture into the realm of the intellect. In "So nicht" (Not this Way), Cain tries to climb back into Paradise over a ladder, but the devil knocks it down. Father Adam remarks to his son: "That serves you right. That's not the way to get into Paradise" (4.412). "The philosophical balloon does not rise beyond the earth atmosphere" is one of the "sprigs" that was not developed into a poem (4.542). And in a reference to his early enthusiasm for Darwin and Schopenhauer, Busch wrote in 1894: "Something like that gradually wanes. Their keys do fit many doors in the enchanted castle of this world; but no 'local' key, and be it the ascetic's key, ever fits the exit door" (4.210).

CHAPTER 5

Fragments of a Great Confession: Busch's Prose Tales

I *Life as a Dream:* Edward's Dream *(1891)*

WHEN Eduard Daelen published *Über Wilhelm Busch und seine Bedeutung* (On Wilhelm Busch and His Significance) in May 1886, Busch was embarrassed. This first extensive study of his work lavished excessive praise on him, ranking him with Dante, Michelangelo, Shakespeare, and Goethe. Furthermore, he was seen chiefly as a political propagandist, as Bismarck's literary and artistic comrade in arms in the *Kulturkampf. Pater Filucius* was consequently depicted as the culmination of his work. Busch's response was an autobiographical essay, "Was mich betrifft" (As Far as I Am Concerned), which appeared in the *Frankfurter Zeitung* in October. The apologetic first paragraph explains why the author decided to share a portion of his private world with the general audience: "It seems peculiar, but because others have written about me, I must do so, too, for once. I cannot fool the reader, who also knows his own heart so profoundly, into believing that I do so reluctantly; that it will be short will come as a pleasant surprise for him" (4.147).

The essay relates a minimum of biographical facts, but offers little insight into Busch's inner life and few comments on his work. In a later revision of 1893, and especially in the final version of 1894, "Von mir über mich" (By Me About Me), statements about family and friends in the original account are further reduced or eliminated. The increasing reluctance to share anything from his private sphere is evident.[1] Much of the concrete information is presented not as an objective and consistent report in chronological order, but as a series of vividly told individual episodes. Isolated events and personalities appear as if fixed in instant photographs. This technique of dissolving a continuous narrative into a

127

sequence of separate images is that of the successful picture stories. And the graphic artist and painter in Busch translated much of what he had to say into visual representations, a trend that can be seen in his poetry as well.

Busch's attempt to assume the stance of an uninvolved observer also affected his style. The subjective self of the writer is often eliminated by the use of the passive voice; or the impersonal "one" is substituted as the subject, thereby transforming a personal observation into a universal condition. Toward the end of the original essay, in a brief discussion of Busch's social habits, the first person is replaced by the third, and the reference is to "the author." Quite consistently, the sequel that appeared in December (not incorporated into the revised versions) is largely told in the third person—and occasionally in the second person, forcing the reader to assume the narrator's identity. The technique of translating reflections into genre scenes or still photographs is intensified. Since the bare facts of his biography had already been told, there was no need for chronological order in this second series of miniatures from various phases of his life.

Busch had considered further sequels to "As Far as I Am Concerned." Instead he decided on a different format that allowed for even greater distancing. The autobiographical essays and his two prose tales complement each other to form a mosaic portrait of Wilhelm Busch in the last decades of his life. What Goethe once said about his own works is equally true for Busch's writings, especially his prose pieces: they all represent but "fragments of a great confession."

Eduards Traum (Edward's Dream) appeared in April 1891, in the same format as *Kritik des Herzens*. Busch once again surprised his audience by switching to a new genre: a prose narrative without illustrations. Many readers must have been bewildered by this series of dream visions which the fictional hero shares with his equally puzzled listeners. Busch anticipated the inability of the average reader to recognize more than a succession of grotesque and entertaining vignettes, as a letter to Lenbach shows: "Thank you very much for your kind words about my little chitchat on printing paper. There will not be many like you whose innate perception is so keen that a soft whisper is enough for their thoughtful amusement" (B, 1.331).

The concluding paragraph of the story seems deceptively defensive. The unobtrusiveness of books is compared with pictures that cannot be ignored as they stare at the viewer from the wall, or with music whose sound cannot be avoided. But the final sentences show that Busch was quite aware of the fact that his tale might be disquieting. He compared a closed book to a "bound, sleeping, harmless little animal. If you don't wake it up, it will not yawn at you; if you don't actually stick your nose between its jaws, it will not bite you" (4.201).

At first glance, Busch appears to be in the tradition of the Romantic movement by selecting the medium of a dream to express his views; and his book has indeed been regarded as a Romantic work.[2] Yet the world as depicted in the narrator's dream is decidedly not Romantic. The people described are characterized by greed, dishonesty, hypocrisy, prejudice, brutality, and lack of affection for one another. There is emphasis on the dark aspects of a self-satisfied society, proud of its accomplishments and confident of future progress. Intellectual achievements and activities in art and literature are seen as shallow and meaningless. The unflattering view of bourgeois Germany at the end of the age of Bismarck, presented by an uninvolved observer, shows Busch in the mainstream of Realism, while some of his narrative techniques point forward to the twentieth century.

It is quite in line with Realist tendencies—as well as with Busch's striving for greater distance—that the author very carefully establishes a separate identity for his protagonist. Edward, a husband and father, tells his dream to his friends; and Busch, the lifelong bachelor, makes himself one of Edward's listeners by referring to the audience in the first person plural. The frame technique, popular during the period of Realism in German literature and frequently employed in the novellas of Storm, Meyer, and Keller, lends authenticity and objectivity to the narrative by making the author appear as a reporter, rather than creator, of his fiction. At the same time, this technique allows for the vividness of a first-person account.

The distancing effect is further increased by having Edward relate not direct personal experience, but a dream for which neither he nor the author can be held responsible. Anticipating the view that was to become commonplace after the findings of Freud and Jung, Busch stressed the lack of control that rational thinking exerts over the content of dreams, "which, after all, are nothing but the dubious amusements in the children's and servants' quarters of the brain after the father and master of the house has gone

to bed" (4.159). The reader is repeatedly reminded of the fact that
Edward is dreaming because when he, during his nocturnal rov-
ings, attempts to pronounce words that contain harsh sounds—
such as the name of a Polish traveler, or the imitation of the
creaking of a weather vane—a voice intrudes from the outside:
"Edward, don't snore like that!"

But Busch's effort to place distance between himself and his
creation went even further. Edward also experiences a change that
makes it possible for him to look at himself from the outside. About
to fall asleep, he extinguishes the candle on the nightstand and for
a moment concentrates on the afterimage of the light. This leads to
a strange sensation: his mind begins to contract, his "intellectual
self" becomes smaller and smaller until he has shrunk to a dot. But
the dot is capable of perception, thought, and motion. Busch
poked gentle fun at Kant's a priori concept of space and time: "I
was not merely a dot, I was a thinking dot. And I was active, too. I
was not only one and two, but I had been there and now I was
here. I thus created my own needs in terms of space and time,
quite in passing, as a by-product, so to speak" (4.160). After a
quick glance into the mirror in order to find out whether he is still
"capable of reflection," Edward decides to travel.

His journey starts in the "Land of Numbers" where he visits an
"arithmetic town" and then proceeds to an "indefinite area." He
attends the festivities of the colony of dots before entering the
"Geometric Plain" and its two-dimensional city. The "Third Di-
mension" is the last stage of the mathematical segment of his trip.
The region of separate parts of the body—heads, hands, legs—
serves as a transition to the world of contemporary human beings
whom the "thinking dot" can observe, but with whom he is unable
to communicate. The countryside is visited first. Far from being
idyllic, it is depicted as populated by cruel and selfish people: a
farmer who loses his wife as the result of an accident and subsequent medical treatment is more concerned about the doctor's
fee than about the death of his spouse, but the sight of his prosper-
ing pigs quickly consoles him. Another shows equal disregard for
his wife while she is still alive; a third mistreats his family after his
return from the tavern. A home is set on fire for the sake of the
insurance money. Other villagers are foolish, dishonest, or preten-
tious.

The city does not offer a more encouraging sight. The description starts with the various desperate persons who end their lives

under the wheels of a passing express train. A brief dialogue between mother and daughter shows the artificiality of communication in this society. The funeral of a respected but dishonest banker leads to glances at business activities. A discussion of attitudes toward Jews follows. The house of an anti-Semite is the setting for a number of genre scenes demonstrating morality and social customs: a young lady is waiting for her fiancé with nitric acid; a couple has a bitter argument at the dinner table; another, after almost fifty years of marriage, has only invectives left as a substitute for communication; a baby-sitter steals from the child in her care; a cashier relaxes after having just invented a "chiaroscuro type of bookkeeping" to hide his embezzlement. Science and art seem to flourish, but a closer look is disillusioning, for the scholars and scientists in the "Temple of Science" are engaged in meaningless research, "pulverizing everything: God, spirit, and Goethe" (4.180). The low quality of literature and art is equally obvious. The citizens are completely disinterested in politics and pay no attention when far-reaching changes occur. A man tries to practice communism by sharing all he has with others, but he is taken advantage of and abused. Another one is touched by his own generosity when he gives a small amount of money to charity.

Edward joins a balloonist on his way up and watches the man rush back to earth when his parachute does not open. The aeronaut, an anti-Semite, has an unpleasant landing on the lightning rod of a synagogue, while Edward's dream self continues to rise into outer space from where earth looks "like a not insignificant dumpling, larded with pieces of white bread" (4.185). Upon his return, he finds himself in an unknown region where people are capable of seeing him and of communicating with him. The society he observes seems ideal: science has solved the problems of energy and food; total equality of all citizens has been achieved; medical research has discovered the "competition gland" whose surgical removal is obligatory for all. Therefore jealousy and envy have disappeared. There is no more need for religion and for the Ten Commandments. But laughter, which is substantially based on the recognition of inequality, has also vanished. As a consequence of the well-regulated monotony of life under such conditions, suicide has become epidemic.

Edward pays a visit to a "world-famous natural philosopher" in order to learn about the true nature of things. He witnesses various demonstrations, but the wise man is not able to provide all the answers, and Edward moves on. There is heavy traffic on a wide highway: everybody is traveling to the "Merry Hind Foot Tavern," run by a jovial innkeeper who walks with a limp and by his seven charming daughters nicknamed "The Seven Deadly Sins." All guests have a wonderful time, but when Edward watches the scene from atop the weather vane, he sees that they are all carted away into a dark tunnel during the night.

The last part of the dream narrative is devoted to Edward's attempts to reach the wondrous "Mountain City." He first travels in the company of four wanderers who have the same goal. But Willich, Wolltich, Wennaber, and Wohlgemut (Will, Would, Butif, and Cheerful), who identify themselves as "Good Intentions," tire of the journey and—each in his own way—give up and slide down the mountain to enjoy themselves in the tavern in the valley. Edward meets other discouraged climbers on their way down and passes an unfortunate man in a cave who is tied in such a way that all he can see is the shadow of whatever goes past on the outside. Edward also observes the attempts to overcome life by self-castigation, meditation, and passivity.

He comes to a meadow where many little black devils are running around with nets, trying to catch butterflies. The gate of a castle opens; a great number of tiny babies emerge and start playing in the grass. The devils join them, and as the result of their romping about, each child gets a little black mark before being picked up and carried away by a stork.

As the "thinking dot" moves on, he sees several quiet pilgrims who have been climbing up the mountain on a different, narrow path. When he wants to join them, he is told: "Poor stranger! You don't have a heart!" The speaker passes through a narrow gate in the wall that resists Edward's efforts to enter. He is only able to cast a glance at the beautiful temple city behind the wall. But he cannot reach his goal because another wall of transparent crystal rises into the sky. Like a fly on a windowpane, Edward moves up and down, then falls to the ground in exhaustion. As he looks up, he sees one of the black devils coming with his net. In desperation, he finds refuge in the open mouth of a sleeping giant who looks strangely familiar.

He regains consciousness in a little room in the attic with two windows that show the light of a new day dawning. There are pictures on the walls that have little similarity with what they are to represent. Still in a daze, Edward goes down the dark stairs and opens the door to a dimly lit room with red curtains where he sees the most beautiful of all women sitting on a golden throne—his wife Elise. That is the moment when he finally awakens from his dream, happy to have his heart back.

Edward's dream visions are told in strict chronological order. This approach results in the occasional reemergence of characters who had been introduced earlier and who thus provide a logical—and sometimes causal—connection between otherwise isolated scenes. At the public dance of the dots, Edward first encounters the "purely mathematical point." As he moves on to the horizontal plane, the point comes along in order to see whether its prospects are better in the world of geometry. Through skillful movement in the two-dimensional world, it soon becomes a voluminous circle. They meet once again in the three-dimensional space, where the shy point, by means of similar manipulations, has developed into an arrogant sphere. A cause-and-effect chain of events leads from three lively flies to the gradual dismemberment of a farmer's wife by an eager doctor who puts his fee into his money purse. Later Edward observes a broom-maker who finds it in the dust and keeps it for himself. We meet the doctor again, whose unhappiness over his loss quickly gives way to a mood of peace and cheer when he witnesses an accident that requires his professional services: a farmer, carried away by the view of his potato fields in the mild light of the setting sun, is run over by a coach. The victim of the mishap is eventually one of the happy guests in the devil's tavern, together with the rich man who was so proud of his generosity. As Edward passes the city jail, he watches the arrival of the villager whose farm he had seen burn. Thus, what first seems a mosaic of unrelated impressions emerges as a carefully constructed nexus.

The events are presented in rapid succession. Busch explained: "A fast verbal pace seemed beneficial to me. Stylistic leisureliness, as it is common in these parts, could easily have made the thing inappropriately thick" (B, 1.331). It is this fast narrative pace—together with the surrealist quality of some of the scenes—that makes *Eduards Traum* appear so modern today.

Even though Busch claimed that it would be difficult to find personal allusions in the story, the autobiographical aspects are evident. Bohne calls this book an answer to the question about the origin and growth of Wilhelm Busch's world view. "From the initial reflections about time and space to the point where no meditation can help any further, the path of the thinking artist has been symbolically retraced in the great journey undertaken by Edward's dream self, condensed into a thinking dot."[3]

The first stages of Edward's travels parallel the traditional sequence of mathematical instruction, from simple arithmetic to its application to business problems, from two-dimensional geometry to three dimensions, from point via circle to sphere.[4] Edward's disenchantment with the mathematical regions is reminiscent of the experience of the engineering student who decided to leave Hanover to become a painter: "So, without bothering to say good-bye, I took an elegant side leap through the wooden wall behind which, as I thought, lay the complete world" (4.168). Yet, Busch found less than the "complete world" at the Düsseldorf Academy. Edward's next sentence reflects that disappointment: "Es war aber nur Stückwerk" ("But it was only fragmentary"). Instead of whole people, he meets heads, hands, and feet separately.

The "friendly village" that Edward inspects could be that of Max and Moritz or Baldwin Baalamb. Busch's observations of his native region are condensed here into a depressing picture of rural life. But the portrait of the city is hardly more positive. In Munich and Frankfort he had had a chance to study all aspects of urban civilization. He had certainly witnessed the loneliness and despair of the big city. Edward's first impression of the "Christian" city he visits is that of desperate people. Both theme and style are surprisingly modern. He sees several individuals on the railroad embankment: "An old man without hope, a woman without a hat, a gambler without money, two lovers without prospects, and two little girls with poor report cards. After the train had passed, the lineman came and collected the heads. He already had a nice basketful in his home" (4.176).

Busch's repeated stays in Frankfort had provided him with some insight into business and banking activities. The city's population had a comparatively large Jewish segment and could furnish material for a case study in anti-Semitism. Traditionally, Christian hostility toward Jews had been especially strong in Frankfort, and it prevailed there longer than elsewhere because the vigorous Jewish competition in commerce and finance was seen as a threat to the ruling bourgeoisie. Busch, who had previously satirized the stereotype resulting from anti-Jewish attitudes, now tried to shed some light on the roots of prejudice. The Jewish characteristics listed would be considered admirable if found among gentiles: the "Israelite" displays "beautiful consistency." He exercises great care in selecting his "kalleh," his bride, but once he has chosen he tends to stay with her under all circumstances and does not change wives frequently "like the others." He goes to bed sober when "the others" are still drinking, and as a result, he gets up early and is alert "when the others are still sleepy." He is clever and does not give up easily if he thinks he can earn something. The reaction of his competitors is predictable: "It goes without saying, however, that one does not become much more popular than rats and mice through such middle-class virtues" (4. 177). In order to make his point even more clearly, Busch had Edward continue by saying that "incidentally," he was above the house of an anti-Semitic contractor at that very moment. The descriptions of the different apartments there are a devastating indictment of the greed, dishonesty, and lack of love to be found in the "Christian" world.

Munich could supply the models for the vignettes of painters and their works as well as their critics. The "man with the dirty glasses" probably represents Friedrich Theodor Vischer, who had attacked Busch's "pornographic stroke" in *Der heilige Antonius.* He is the critic who "smells everywhere the filth that he himself is bringing along." Another critic, "with a face as malicious as that of a thousand-year-old raven," complains about the absence of "complete human beings" among the artists. Their subservient behavior toward him—while they call him a fool behind his back—shows the power he wields because "fear is the name of the author of everybody's book of compliments" (4.181).

Contemporary music and literature are also reviewed by the "thinking dot." Hermann Levi, who was devoting his life to the promotion of Richard Wagner's music, had tried in vain to instill in his friend enthusiasm for the compositions of his musical idol. Busch maintained a cool distance, even after meeting the composer. Wagner's music is satirized as Edward endures a concert by ninety-seven toads, three hundred and forty-four water frogs, and two thousand two hundred and twenty-two crickets. When Edward praises the "musical rrrrevelation," Elise's voice intrudes from the outside, telling him not to snore.

Busch's references to literature in *Eduards Traum* are both general and specific. Edward comments on the skill of some of the "separate hands," one of whom is a barber who knows how to make much lather from little soap. He has recently become a literary man and is so successful that he is already wearing three diamond rings on each finger. This description might fit any successful but shallow writer.

But Busch left little doubt as to the literary movement he was ridiculing when Edward tells about his experience in the theater. The play he saw was "newly imported" and featured "cruelly natural" action. Afterwards, several writers, "who also had always been determined to do something without really knowing what," sing their enthusiastic praise of the new literature of the "natural." The comment following this scene is a serious attempt to define the essence of art, but it is expressed in the grotesque form of a culinary image. It summarizes the author's attitude toward his own work and also explains why he could not appreciate the Naturalist movement that was just beginning to emerge in German literature. Edward compares a work of art to sauerkraut: it "should be cooked on the fire of nature, then placed in the pantry cupboard of memory, then reheated three times in the golden pan of imagination, then served by well-shaped hands, and finally it should be consumed in gratitude with a hearty appetite" (4.179).

Eduards Traum demonstrates the diversity of Busch's interests. He uses Homer's *Odyssey* to show that sirens in the age of capitalism need golden eggs in order to be seductive—but their gold is not even genuine. By means of Plato's cave parable he emphasizes that man's intellect is not an adequate tool to comprehend the world, and that no number of reincarnations will improve human understanding. He ridicules the theory that language grew out of interjections, the "pooh-pooh Theory," as F. Max Müller had called it in 1861: two peasant boys fight while uttering the sounds of the vowels. A cock pigeon is tenderly cooing "Nurdu, nurdu" ("onlyyou, onlyyou") to his mate when a hawk puts an end to that idyll with a triumphant "Teehee!" As Edward starts to formulate his insight, "The orrrigin of language . . . ," he is told by the voice from the outside to stop snoring (4.170).

There are passing references to solar energy, to the synthetic production of sugar, and to the ether theory of wave propagation, current at the time. Busch returned to Darwin's theory but gave it an ironic twist to bring it into line with Schopenhauer's belief in the continuous return of the will. The natural philosopher shows Edward that modern man is not the highest form of development but represents a phase in a new evolutionary cycle after a much higher form of existence had gradually degenerated into the primitive stage of a lancelet. The inescapable conclusion is that this degeneration will repeat itself—a view that certainly was not in accord with nineteenth-century optimism.

Clearly Busch was rather skeptical of man's ability to find answers to human problems, even if scientific solutions could be discovered. His glimpse of the future, with suicides dangling from every tree in a society that ought to be happy, is depressing. He did not see how political developments could assure a better future for mankind, either. The resignation of Bismarck in March 1890, and the apathy of the people, prompted Edward's comment: "A few days ago, the greatest man of his nation had stepped down from the driver's seat and had relinquished the reins of the world. Now you would have expected a lot of rumble and helter-skelter. But no! . . . The world is like porridge. If you pull out the spoon, even the biggest one, the whole mess collapses again as if nothing had happened at all" (4.181–82).

The episode of Edward's search for a "truly good man" is certainly meant as a political statement. The "conspicuous philanthropist," who finds possessions a burden, invites five wanderers from the road into his villa and offers to share with them everything he has. After a short time, his guests mistreat him and throw him out of his own house. A writer who agreed with Schopenhauer's pessimistic view of mankind, and who did not believe in man's ability to overcome his innate selfishness, could surely not see socialism and the sharing of wealth as possible.

Philosophy is not immune from satire in *Eduards Traum*. Busch pokes fun at some of the teachings of Kant and Leibniz. Edward produces his "own needs in terms of space and time," and the natural philosopher shows him Kant's "thing-in-itself": a little electric fan capable of creating what Kant called the "phenomena" and what Edward experiences as sensory perceptions. A similarly grotesque translation of a philosophical concept into very concrete terms occurs when the traveler joins the frolicking dots at their dance. One of the female dots looks very familiar to him. He finally recognizes her as Leibniz's "old Monad," now quite rejuvenated. When she "clasps her scrawny valences" around him and suggests that they cling to each other for all eternity, Edward leaves the scene as fast as he can (4.165).

In passing, Schopenhauer's suggestion of the possibility of self-salvation through renunciation of the will is ridiculed once more in the man who has been sitting in the same spot for a long time because, as he claims, "Life is a debt! I am sitting it out!" (4.197).[5] Even more direct is the reference to Schopenhauer in one of the demonstrations by the natural philosopher. Schopenhauer had, on various occasions, proposed a seemingly paradoxical reversal of the common reactions to happiness and pain, perhaps most succinctly in his "Aphorisms." He pointed to the fact that we are keenly aware of anything that is opposed to our will and thus creates an unpleasant or painful experience: we do not feel the health of our entire body, but only the little spot where our shoe pinches. This is the basis of the negativity of well-being and happiness in contrast to the positivity of pain. What we call "good" is merely the termination of a desire or a pain.[6] Edward is placed in the "easy chair of higher sensitivity" in order to be able to have normal sensations despite his lack of physical substance. When the philosopher turns a certain screw, Edward feels intense pain (as if his old great-aunt had died). The master explains: "Pain is positive!" and then turns the screw in the other direction. The pain subsides (as if the death had resulted in an inheritance of half a million): "Joy is negative!" (4.190).

The natural philosopher cannot give Edward a clear response to his question concerning man's ethical behavior and disappears into his back room crowing like a rooster. The traveler moves on from the sphere of human thought into the symbolic landscape of faith. This transition—and the change in focus connected with it—is significant. In 1875 Busch had written, "Our philosophy after our thirtieth year is called *faith*" (B, 1.137). Up to this point in the tale, the "thinking dot" had moved through the world of human folly as a curious, but largely uninvolved note-taker, just like Jonathan Swift's Gulliver. In both stories, the grotesque universe is described by an observer whose size and physical attributes set him apart from its inhabitants. But it actually constitutes a caricature of contemporary society as the authors saw it. As Edward leaves the philosopher's study, he gradually changes from a mere spectator to an active pursuer of a specific goal. As a pilgrim, he attempts to reach the temple city high in the clouds. Various sights along the way to the top of the mountain are being left behind because they seem of no use to him. *Gulliver's Travels* and its social satire could not provide the model for this concluding part of *Eduards Traum*. It was, rather, furnished by another English book with which Busch was familiar, John Bunyan's *The Pilgrim's Progress*.

The impact of Bunyan's allegory can be seen in the general concept of the last segment of Edward's journey. There are also some parallels in narrative technique, and a few details in Busch's tale might be traced to the devotional book written more than two centuries earlier. Both authors use the fiction of a dream vision; and the exhausting and dangerous pilgrimage of "Christian" to the "Celestial City" probably inspired Edward's ascent toward the same goal, although it is possible that both accounts are based on the same Biblical passages.[7] Bunyan's consistent use of allegorical names, such as "Good-will," "Feeble-mind," and "Ready-to-halt," is echoed in the names of the four "Good Intentions" who give up their pilgrimage and slide down the mountain into the devil's tavern. The English narrative has several examples of the rapid descent into hell, and the "Merry Hind Foot Tavern" with its jovial host and his daughters who do their best to discourage people from taking the path up the mountain are reminiscent of Bunyan's "Enchanted Ground" and Madam Bubble and her daughters. Bunyan's method of translating theological concepts into tangible characters and events must have appealed to Busch who used pictures instead of abstract arguments whenever he could. His visualization of the idea of original sin in the form of the black marks which the yet unborn babies receive when they romp around with the little devils is quite in the spirit of *The Pilgrim's Progress*.

But there is one important difference. Christian reaches his goal, and later Christiana, his wife, succeeds in the same undertaking. The "thinking dot," however, can only look at the beautiful city beyond the wall. When Christiana crosses the river to enter the holy place, Mr. Great-heart and Mr. Valiant-for-truth play "upon the well-tuned cymbal and harp for joy."[8] When Edward falls to the ground in exhaustion after having failed to scale the wall, there is a ringing noise like a "sounding cymbal." Busch put the expression in quotation marks, and it not only calls to mind Bunyan's formulation; more importantly, it paraphrases 1 Corinthians 13:1: "Though I speak with the tongues of men and of angels, and have not charity, I am become as sounding brass, or a tinkling cymbal." Edward had been told that he had no heart. This lack of heart and charity keeps him out of the celestial city despite any other qualifications he might have. As Busch showed in his poem, Cain could not climb back into Eden on a ladder. The failure of Edward's "intellectual self" to enter the City of God—which is also unattainable to Bunyan's Mr. Worldly-wise-man—is an affirmation of Busch's belief that the castle of faith cannot be penetrated by intellect. In 1881 he had written to Levi: "The conversation we once started somewhere near a church ought not to be over yet; but I already know One thing: nobody will pass through the strait gate by being just a high-minded civilized person" (B, 1.221).

Wolfgang Kayser, who called *Eduards Traum* Busch's "most perfect grotesque," was right in suggesting that one could assign a meaning to the entire sequence on the basis of its conclusion.[9] The world depicted in the story is one without a heart, without kindness or love. This is the perception of an observer devoid of feeling, but to some extent it also reflects Busch's own view. Yet the author clearly saw the limitations of such a perspective. When Edward's thinking self returns to his sleeping body, he first finds himself in the small attic room. Edward looks at his own head from the inside and recognizes that the mental pictures on the walls do not reflect reality any more distinctly than did the shadows on the wall of the prisoner's mountain cave. By going down the stairs into the realm of emotions, into the "dimly lit room" with the red curtains, Edward can relate to others again. Contrary to Kayser's interpretation, Edward's thoughts upon awakening and seeing his wife and son again do not have to be taken as satirizing human kindness, but could constitute an affirmation of the concept of a whole person, acknowledging the importance of the heart as well as that of the mind.[10] Only a whole person can reach the final insight that Edward has gained through his dream and that he shares with his listeners, the realization that we are all no good.

This admission was certainly not easy for the self-satisfied bourgeois at the end of the century. The reaction of Edward's audience is a response not only to the social and cultural criticism presented in the tale, but perhaps even more so to the personal consequences suggested by it: "Wir waren auch sonst nicht so befriedigt, wie es wohl wünschenswert. Wir hatten doch mancherlei Dinge vernommen, die dem Ohre eines feinen Jahrhunderts recht schmerzlich sind. Wozu so was? Und dann ferner. Warum gleich lumpig einhergehn und es jedermann merken lassen, daß die Bilanzen ein Defizit aufweisen? Würde es nicht vielmehr schicklich und vorteilhaft sein, sich fein und patent zu machen, wie es der Kredit des 'Hauses' erfordert, dem als Teilhaber anzugehören wir sämtlich die Ehre haben?" ("In other ways, too, we were not as satisfied as would be desirable. We had listened to many things that are rather painful to the ear of a refined century. What is the use of all that? And furthermore. Why run around in rags and demonstrate to everybody that the balance sheet shows a deficit? Wouldn't it rather be appropriate and advantageous to dress up elegantly and splendidly, as the credit of the 'firm' requires whose partners we all have the honor of being?") (4.201).

While twentieth-century readers may still find Edward's insight "painful," their acceptance of it has been made easier by Kafka's grotesque nightmares and by the Surrealist concept of an absurd world that defies intellectual comprehension. The "little chitchat on printing paper" appears astonishingly modern today, since most of the observations are as pertinent now as they were at the end of the last century.

II   *Life as a Fairy Tale:* The Butterfly *(1895)*

When Busch offered Bassermann *Der Schmetterling* (The Butterfly), he referred to it as a "counterpart to Edward's Dream" and suggested that the twenty-one small drawings be incorporated into the text in the manner of books printed in bygone centuries (B, 2.45). The pictures in this case were clearly meant as mere illustrations, assuming little function of their own. The delighted publisher brought out the book shortly after Busch's sixty-third birthday. During the author's lifetime, 20,000 copies were sold, twice as many as of *Eduards Traum*. Yet neither of the prose tales could ever reach the popularity of the successful picture stories. Only very few sensitive readers of *Der Schmetterling* attempted to seek for deeper meaning in what seemed to be an entertaining fairy tale, presented in simple but precise language and containing a number of vividly portrayed characters and colorful scenes. Even today not much critical attention is given to what some scholars have called Busch's "most remarkable work" or the "poetic apex of his oeuvre."[11]

Der Schmetterling is the first-person account of the life story of Peter, who leaves his father's farm one summer day and returns home after many years, a beggar and a cripple. Peter was born "not far from the good town of Geckelbeck." His mother had died early; the household was now run by his pretty cousin Katherine. Trusty Gottlieb, the farmhand, helped Peter's father with the daily chores. Since the boy did not show any inclination toward farm work, he was sent to town to get an education—an attempt that was as unsuccessful as was his apprenticeship with a tailor, which merely resulted in a new suit of clothes, blue tailcoat and yellow trousers, his attire throughout the story.

Peter spends his time around the farm chasing butterflies in the summer, watching Katherine at work in the winter, or sitting in his attic room reading an old book of legends until late at night. He often sees witches riding their brooms past his window. Most of them are old and ugly, but one is young and pretty, with a chain of gold coins in her hair, and with her white teeth shining as she smiles at him. This is Lucinda, and her spell over him is one of the important motifs of the story, the other being his pursuit of the elusive butterfly that lures him so far from his home that he cannot find his way back.

The fabric of the story is made up of his adventures during the years of trying to catch the beautiful insect. Most episodes result in unpleasant or painful situations for Peter, who walks through life with the naive innocence of Wolfram von Eschenbach's Parzival. His chase leads him into a pond of leeches, into a hollow tree crawling with ants, and to an encounter with an angry ghost that drops him from the height of a church spire, thus inducing a seven-year sleep. Vainly Peter seeks to obtain information about the way back to his hometown from the many unusual characters he meets: a blind man, a deaf-mute, a town crier whose fading memory he can restore, a talkative swineherd who calmly watches as his pigs almost chew off the ears of sleeping Peter. He visits villages populated by lazy people or by those who cannot be serious about anything. An argument with an arrogant beggar costs him a front tooth, but that loss enables him to whistle even better. He remains undaunted in other adversities too, such as his fall into the bedroom of an unsuspecting family, when the loft where he had found shelter for the night collapses. Whenever necessary, he can earn some money or food through the skills acquired as a tailor's apprentice.

The periodic appearance of a few individuals adds consistency to the loose structure of the tale. Peter first meets Nazi, a young man who is at the time accompanied by a snake. The reptile shows an obvious interest in the golden locket on Peter's chest. Later Peter finds Nazi hanging from a tree. He cuts him down and revives the would-be suicide, who shows little gratitude and, after a while, tells him about the girl who had left him after taking all his money. The two young men travel together, often begging for food. Peter is appalled by the way Nazi tricks and cheats people, but at the same time cannot really be angry because of his companion's cheerful and charming manner. Their relationship ends very suddenly when Peter comes into some money and Nazi robs him. But there is one last reunion. Peter accepts a ride on the wagon of a happy peasant on his way to town. He discovers that the vehicle is carrying the mortal remains of his friend—who has died of a snakebite—to a doctor's office for dissection.

The money Nazi took from Peter had actually been produced by

the donkey of Schlumann, an old man whose path crosses that of
Peter several times. It was Schlumann who rescued him when he was
trapped in the hollow tree. Schlumann arrived at the place of Peter's
predicament in pursuit of thieves who had stolen his donkey. Peter
had chased away the criminals by his screams when the ants started
attacking him. Some time later it becomes clear why the animal is so
valuable to its possessor. Peter awakens one morning in an isolated
inn and notices a stable next to his room. Through a wide crack in the
wooden wall he watches Schlumann coaxing his donkey into laying
ducats into his hat. Peter cannot resist the temptation to reach
through the crack and gather up some of that money. He meets
Schlumann two more times. The last occasion is a fashionable party
that Peter watches through a window of the palace where it is held.
The old man is host to many elegant people who have come to gamble
in the company of pretty Lucinda and a jovial elderly gentleman with
black face and hands, long nails, crooked nose, pointed ears, and two
cute golden horns on his forehead.

The impact of the witch Lucinda on Peter is one of the clearest
illustrations of the power of Eros in Busch's work. Ever since Peter
saw her outside his window, he has been fascinated by her. It was she
who accompanied Nazi in the form of a snake and who was responsible for his suicide attempt and eventual demise. Peter encounters her
again when he finds shelter in a bower during a heavy storm. She
embraces and kisses the surprised young man. When Peter reaches
for one of the dried pears she has in her apron, the fruits turn into
mice. Lucinda disappears, and Peter's locket is gone, and with it his
memories of home and his desire to return there. They next meet at a
dance in Juxum, the cheerful village. Lucinda dances with him, then
leaves him for a deformed but rich suitor. Peter creates a disturbance
and is thrown out. After the dance he sees the girl at a window
apparently beckoning him to join her. When he follows her invitation, he finds himself trapped by the frame of the window which holds
his arms like a vise. While he is hanging there, Lucinda's friend burns
his nose with a candle, and the happy population of Juxum uses his
posterior as a target for blows and missiles.

Peter sees his opportunity for revenge when he comes upon
Lucinda on a moonlit night as she is bathing in a forest lake. He
seizes the chain of gold coins she had taken off, but suddenly he finds
himself riding through the air on a broom. After an uncomfortable
flight he is deposited in a kitchen. In the morning a very old woman
enters. Peter asks for some salve for his sores, but the result is quite

unexpected: he is turning into a blue poodle with yellow hind legs. The gold coins he had carried in his coat are now jingling in his tail. Instead of the old witch, Lucinda appears and indicates that she will get her coins back when the moon is full again. Peter tries in vain to win the affection of his mistress, who treats him badly and does not feed him. He witnesses how warmly she welcomes Nazi, but their reunion is interrupted when Old Schlumann shows up and is greeted by the girl as her uncle. Nazi, in a fit of jealousy, attacks the old man, but is easily overpowered and thrown out. The furious poodle has an opportunity to tear a large piece out of Nazi's new trousers: Peter has become quite canine in his behavior. He finally runs away in desperation, but eventually, after many adventures, returns to Lucinda whose spell he cannot escape. She seems happy to see him again, offers him good food, and suddenly traps him when he sticks his head into a chest. With a pair of fire tongs, she clips off the end of his tail to get her coins back, thereby returning to him his human form. The tails of his coat are gone. Before he can escape, she blows cold air at him with the bellows; thus his neck stays crooked.

He sees her again when she leaves the gambling party in the company of the dark gentleman. They are riding off in a coach, which is glowing like fiery gold. Following an impulse, Peter tries to jump on its running board, but quickly realizes that the vehicle is red-hot. His right foot is badly burnt and is later amputated by the same jovial doctor who is the recipient of Nazi's body. After he has learned to walk on crutches, the doctor lets him look at himself in the mirror: "I did not like the man I saw in there. Bald head, red nose, crooked neck, scrubby beard; half a tailcoat, half a leg; all in all, a horrible person. And that was I" (4.259–60).

Without noticing it, Peter had retrieved his locket in the chest in Lucinda's house, and the wish to go home becomes very strong in him. He gets to Geckelbeck much faster than expected. Each community he enters considers him undesirable and deports him to the next village until, on a snowy winter evening, he finds himself back at his parental farm. He is invited in by Gottlieb and his wife Katherine, who have inherited the farm from Peter's father. Peter does not identify himself but gives "Fritz Fröhlich" ("Fred Cheerful") as his name. Little Peter, the couple's oldest son, calls him "Humpel-fritze" ("Hobble Freddy"), and soon everybody uses this nickname. He is asked to stay with the family, moves into his old room, and earns his keep by mending and sewing. His odyssey is over: "Und so leb ich denn allhier als ein stilles, geduldiges, nutzbares Haustier.—Schmet-

terlinge beacht ich nicht mehr.—Oben im alten Giebelstüb-
chen hab ich mir eine gemütliche Werkstatt eingerichtet" ("And so I
am living here as a quiet, patient, useful domestic animal.—I don't
pay attention to butterflies anymore.—I have set up a comfortable
workshop for myself upstairs in the old attic") (4.262). The witches are
still riding past. One day, as Peter is writing his story, Lucinda peers
through the window "laughing like crazy." She is still as pretty as
ever. He looks at her calmly, whistles, takes a pinch of snuff, and says
"atchoo!"

Peter's identity is discovered only after his death when his locket is
found. According to a brief epilogue to the story, his manuscript had
been hidden for many years in the pigeon loft next to the attic. The
fictitious editor does not doubt the genuineness of Peter's account,
claiming that his "artless, unaffected style, his completely honest
report of even those experiences that were extremely embarrassing
to him," mark his narrative as truthful. "Only a half-educated person,
who is, of course, not familiar with recent findings of inductive
science in the area of the supernatural, will take exception to this or
that which people in the past used to call impossible" (4.263).

This pseudorationalistic postscript pretends to establish credibility
for the fanciful tale. Coming immediately after the description of the
never-aging witch looking in through the window, the reference to
"recent findings of inductive science" is particularly effective. The
fairy tale of the Romantic movement and the Realism of the second
half of the century confront each other.

At first glance, much of the story seems to conform to the format of
the fairy tale. Peter is the happy-go-lucky simpleton who should
marry the princess in the end. The traditional vagueness of the time
frame seems to have been replaced with more specific references to
the period, but they turn out to be equally vague: "I was born in the
good old days when young ladies were called mademoiselle, and
geese were still named Adelheid" (4.214). The witch Lucinda, the
"dark gentleman" with the "cute golden horns," Old Schlumann and
his miraculous donkey, mischievous Nazi, the lazy inhabitants of
Dösingen, and the merry ones of Juxum are all typical fairy tale
characters. The various magic transformations—Lucinda takes the
shape of a snake, pears turn into mice, and Peter is changed into a
dog—have their counterparts in many folk tales. Even the incident of
Peter's restoring the failing memory of the desperate town crier by
suggesting that the forgotten name might be that of his former
master, Knippipp the tailor, could be interpreted as the traditional

breaking of the magic spell. The loss and retrieval of the golden
locket, with the accompanying loss and restoration of memory, is also
a common motif.

Yet many aspects of the story are alien to the traditional fairy tale. The
"documentary" conclusion is part of the objectifying frame so popular
in German Realism. The pretended authenticity of the first-person
account contrasts with the conventional acceptance of the fairy tale
world as completely fictional. Some of the scenes described by
Busch, and especially the implied psychological motivation, betray the
objective view of a Realist. When young Peter, still at home, pushes a
pin through his ear or balances on the edge of the well in order to
impress Katherine, or when he climbs into the tree outside her
bedroom window to watch her going to bed, we witness incidents that
are based on careful observation of reality.

Even an event that seems to come directly from the fairy tale
tradition, Peter's metamorphosis into a dog, is treated in a most
untraditional form. Busch interjected into the customary enchant-
ment scene the scientific concept of the uniformity of the basic
construction elements of nature that makes possible different forms
through rearrangement. He raised the philosophical question of the
relationship between identity and appearance, and he even presented a psychological interpretation of the transformation by implying that the relative control of the ego over the id distinguishes man
from beast. After having been turned into a poodle, Peter muses:
"Ich—muß ich mich noch so nennen, nach dem, was vorangegangen?
Oder darf ich Er sagen zu mir? Leider nein! so gern ich auch möchte;
denn das fühlt ich genau: Die sämtlichen alten Bestandteile meiner
Natur hatten sich nur verschoben und etwas anders gelagert als
zuvor, und während der untergeordnete Teil meines Verstandes zur
Herrschaft gelangte, war mein höheres Denkvermögen gewisserma-
ßen auf die Leibzucht gezogen, ins Hinterstübel, von wo aus es
immer noch zusah, wie die neue Wirtschaft sich machte, wenn es
auch selbst nichts mehr zu sagen hatte" ("I—must I still call myself
that, after all that happened? Or may I call myself 'He'? Unfortunately not! much as I would like it; because I felt one thing very
clearly: all the component parts of my nature had simply shifted and
had settled in an arrangement somewhat different from before, and
while the subordinate part of my mind had gained control, my higher
reasoning had retired, so to say, had moved into a back room, from
where it could still watch how the new management was working out,
even though it no longer had any say") (4.247).

The recognition of those two different levels within the narrative of *Der Schmetterling* caused Peter Marxer to attempt to distinguish between the world of Peter, realistic and sober, and that of Lucinda, mystical and elusive. Both interact, and the result is a double parody. The sphere of the fairy tale is parodied by the insertion of rational and everyday elements, and Peter finds himself alienated in his workaday world through the intrusion of the irrational, symbolized by the pretty witch. Marxer quotes Dürrenmatt's view of parody as a way for the writer to regain his freedom. Parody for Busch then means free command over two different realms, two different human and artistic attitudes that shape each other.[12] This interpretation permits interesting insights. But the "mutual shaping" or "parodying" in Busch's tale goes so far that it is difficult to separate the two levels at all times. There is also the third realm, represented by the butterfly, of the allegorical and the symbolical, which makes this story a true "counterpart" of *Eduards Traum.*

This third level makes Peter's life story and the fairy tale about Lucinda Busch's personal statement. It would be too narrow a view to see *Der Schmetterling* merely as a poetic autobiography and to try to relate everything in the story to events and specific persons in Busch's life. Yet Peter represents his author as much as Edward did, and some of the parallels in their journeys through life stand out. Busch shared with his protagonist the rural background and, like Peter, he returned to his point of origin after years of trying to find himself. He was sent to the city to receive an education but left school "after just a few years." Busch's father had grudgingly given his approval when his son contemplated a new career, and Peter's father reacts the same way. To hard-working Johann Friedrich Wilhelm Busch his son must have looked occasionally like young Peter, wasting his time with no apparent purpose in life.

Peter unsuccessfully seeks guidance from blind and deaf people, and neither beggar nor swineherd provides any help. Busch may have thought of some of his contemporaries who proved similarly incapable of understanding him or of serving as guides as he was trying to find his own way. Upon his return home, Peter chooses the pseudonym "Fred Cheerful"—a name that suggests society's label for the author of the amusing picture stories. The account of his work in the "comfortable workshop" in the attic is reminiscent of Busch's career that had led from the attempt to collect and preserve folkloristic material to the creation of a new artistic genre and new modes of expression: "Days became weeks, weeks have grown into

years. Through ample practice my skill increased not only in the
restoration of the old and decayed, but I also created new things,
applying my own yardstick and drawing from rich resources" (4.262).
But, as in the case of Busch, the real person behind diligent Fred
Cheerful remained unknown even in subsequent generations.

The chase after the elusive butterfly might symbolize Busch's
pursuit of a painting career that took him away from home and proved
an increasingly unattainable goal. With equal justification, the story
has been interpreted as his rejection of Romanticism in poetry and
philosophy, his "No" to "the so-called Idealism that chases colorful
butterflies without noticing that meanwhile all genuine values of
true, non-Romantic life are being lost."[13]

But Busch seems to indicate that any very specific interpretation of
this motif would be too narrow. Everybody is chasing butterflies, as
the most symbolic scene in the book shows: after sleeping for seven
years, Peter awakens and realizes once more that he is alive as a part
"of this so-called world system whose overview as a whole is really
quite difficult." He finds himself in a garden, surrounded by a high
wall. Next to him is a cabbage field. There are caterpillars on every
cabbage head. Within a few moments, they change into chrysalises,
and then into butterflies. There is also a very high tree, covered with
bird nests from which a great number of black birds emerge. The
cabbage is growing rapidly, and suddenly each head turns into a
human being, butterfly net in hand. As the butterflies disappear over
the wall, birds and people go after them. Only then does Peter notice
two giant bugs, a burying beetle and a scarab, who are cultivating the
field to his left and who are ready to dig him under as fertilizer for the
new crop they want to sow. Peter observes that there seem to be
many more birds than butterflies. The scarab agrees: "Only on the
other side, beyond the wall, do you really notice that. For each
pleasant expectation, there are at least three unpleasant possibilities"
(4.255). The burying beetle tells him to lie still so that they can do
their work when suddenly Peter's butterfly rises from the field, and
once more the human will to live reasserts itself, and with it the
willingness to pursue new ideals, even though they may be destroyed
by reality. "Give me a net!" he shouts, "I want out!" "Who wants to
go, may go!" is the response, and Peter takes a giant leap over the
wall. But just as he is ready to catch his butterfly a black bird snatches
it away.

This symbolic scene and the one immediately following it could
easily have been part of Edward's dream visions. Peter finds himself

outside the palace where the devil's party is taking place. The liveried footmen, waiting for the departure of their masters and mistresses, proudly display various mottoes, embroidered on their uniforms. Peter reads, "Good," "Beautiful," "True," "Ora," and "Labora." The most impressive-looking one among them, "Faithful and Honest," identifies the group as the "Moral Principles." But they are no more reliable than were the "Good Intentions" in *Eduards Traum*: Peter tries to shake the hand of "Faithful and Honest" but finds it "softer than butter," and a friendly pat on the shoulder causes the footman's collapse. The "Moral Principle" is just a bag filled with air.

While these allegorical figures are reminiscent of the other prose tale, many of the episodes throughout the book bring to mind Busch's earlier works. In some cases, motifs used before occur here in a different context. Other scenes read like outlines for never completed picture stories. The pond with leeches; the unexpected fall through the ceiling; two fighting roosters and their possessors, the two young rascals who force Peter to flee into the deceptive safety of the hollow tree; the attacking ants—they all have their counterparts in Busch's previous oeuvre. The unpleasant experience with the children of the grateful town crier is similar to an episode in Knopp's quest for a wife, and Lucinda's luring Peter to climb through her window is modeled after Baldwin Baalamb's misadventure. Other motifs, such as the encounter with the beggar who returns part of the gift to the donor rather than showing gratitude, or the rescue of someone from the gallows who later robs the man who saved him, or Lucinda's mocking of the lightning that missed her, were used in Busch's poetry. The jovial doctor who enjoys performing the amputation is akin to several medical men portrayed by Busch. It is as if the author had tried to incorporate as much of his earlier work as possible into his final narrative.

The amputation scene is instructive for another reason as well. Again Busch made use of sound effects, from the groans of the hard-working surgeon to the noise of the saw, first cutting through flesh and then through bone, to the final "bump" when the severed limb falls to the floor. This extremely realistic treatment of a very unpleasant action comes close to the goals of the Naturalist movement, especially since the brutality of the description is not relieved by the grotesque use of rhyme or meter as it is in many picture stories. But Busch applied other techniques to achieve the same softening effect. The result of the surgery is linguistically alienated by centering on the severed limb rather than its possessor: "Da! Mein

Fuß war mich losgeworden" ("There! My foot had got rid of me")
(4.259). The accompanying illustration further blunts the impact.
Peter's face is not shown; his clenched fist is the only indication of
pain. The doctor is happily sawing away, but sawdust rather than
blood seems to emanate from the wound (Ill. 20).

Other drawings show a similar tendency toward understatement in
contrast to the technique of exaggeration in the picture stories. When
Nazi attacks Schlumann, Lucinda intervenes: "Quick as lightning she
had caught the tip of Nazi's nose between the knuckles of her middle
and index fingers and twisted it into a painful spiral" (4.249). In *Fipps
der Affe*, Busch had used almost the identical wording. In the picture
story the unpleasant transformation of the monkey catcher's nose had
been drastically demonstrated in three consecutive drawings (Ill. 21).
In *Der Schmetterling*, the gruesome detail is omitted from the
illustration; we merely see a helpless Nazi being led out of the room
by his nose (Ill. 22).

Like Peter, Busch had returned to his point of departure. His
narrative work had started with the prose tale about skaters during a
severe winter. Folklore had provided the source, and his rural
environment had furnished the setting. The picture that accompanied the story had depicted one of the less dramatic moments and
was clearly designed as a mere illustration for the grotesque account.
In *Der Schmetterling*, the format is almost identical, even though the
sophistication and the scope of this tale go far beyond the modest
humorous yarn of thirty-six years earlier. Perhaps Busch "had run in a
circle only," but that circular path had yielded a lifetime of experience, and *Der Schmetterling* is the reflection of that experience.

Peter's reference to himself as a "quiet, patient, useful domestic
animal" could be read as an expression of bitterness on the part of the
author. But that interpretation would overlook the sentiment expressed in the introductory passage. While *Eduards Traum*
suggested the ultimately unsuccessful attempt to find intellectual
answers, *Der Schmetterling* starts out from Edward's final insight:
"Children, in their innocence, ask again and again: Why? A wise
person does not do that anymore because he has long since learned
that each Why is only the end of a thread that leads into the thick
tangle of infinity, with which nobody can really cope, regardless of
how much winding and reeling he may do" (4.213).

This is what Peter has learned from his years of chasing the
butterfly, and this is the final observation of the aging author: "Years

ago, to be sure, as I was taking the little excursion about which more will be said below, I often pondered why all this had to happen to me of all people, such a nice and outstanding man. Now I am sitting here in calm composure and softly whistle for myself while simply assuming: what has been decided in the council of all things ought to be appropriate and beneficial" (4.213).

"Fred Cheerful's" final acceptance of things as they are establishes an important parallel between *Der Schmetterling* and a work, written almost seventy years earlier, which is often seen as the epitome of the Romantic movement in Germany. Joseph von Eichendorff's novella, *Aus dem Leben eines Taugenichts (From the Life of a Good-for-Nothing)*, seems to have served as a model for Busch. Both books are parodies of the traditional *Entwicklungsroman*. The Romantic writer also utilizes a fairy tale setting for his first-person account of a lighthearted young man's adventures after leaving his father's rural home. Peter shares several characteristics with his predecessor. Both continue their journeys undaunted after each mishap, and both frequently find themselves in situations they do not understand. A healthy constitution, manifesting itself in the ability to fall asleep under almost any circumstances, contributes to each man's continued strength. Both eventually return home even though the circumstances differ greatly.

Good-for-Nothing and Peter like music, but their respective ways of performing clearly illustrate the transition from Romanticism to Realism: Eichendorff's hero plays the violin; Busch's protagonist whistles through a missing front tooth. Similarly, other motifs from the earlier tale appear in *Der Schmetterling* in significantly changed form. The Romantic traveler escapes from an isolated castle where he had been royally entertained with food and wine. Peter and Nazi contemplate fleeing from an isolated inn through the window because they cannot pay for the good food and beer they consumed, but they are frustrated by the innkeeper who confiscates their trousers. When Good-for-Nothing jumps onto a beautiful young lady's carriage, he is able to travel right into a castle in Vienna. Peter's similar venture results in the loss of his foot. And while Eichendorff's hero eventually marries his "lovely and gracious lady" whom he had followed throughout the story, Peter stays single and watches Lucinda through his attic window.

Peter's path was thornier than that of his Romantic counterpart. In the end, he no longer pays any attention to butterflies: the Romantic age is over. But his reference to the decision "in the council of all things," and his final sneeze, amount to the observation with which Eichendorff's protagonist had concluded his account: "And everything, everything was good."

CHAPTER 6

A Concluding Note: Busch and His Public

WILHELM Busch's popularity in the German-speaking countries remains undiminished. He is probably the most widely quoted author, and there are few Germans who do not know one or more of his picture stories. The great number of Busch parodies attests to the public's familiarity with his work. Political cartoonists often utilize his characters for caricatures of individual politicians or even a whole society, as in the elaborate parody by Klaus Budzinski and Rainer Hachfeld, *Marx und Maoritz.*[1]

But much of this popularity is based on the audience's continuing inability to see more in Busch than a humorous entertainer. This label has stayed with him from the time of his first contributions to Braun's publications, and, as a consequence, a significant segment of his work is still ignored by the average reader. The comparative lack of interest literary scholars have shown in this author results from the same one-sided image. Ever since the publication of *Max und Moritz,* Busch has been categorized as a children's author.[2] Some of the accusations of sadism have been prompted by this classification. The politicizing of his work has not stopped with Daelen's book. National Socialist propaganda misused his social satire for anti-Semitic and antireligious purposes. What the Nazis depicted as a virtue in the author was held against him after 1945, and when the editor of a two-volume set of Busch's works, Rolf Hochhuth, published his controversial drama *The Deputy,* attacks were leveled against Busch by Catholic critics who were actually seeking to discredit Hochhuth. At the same time, Communist critics have consistently praised Busch's satiric view of bourgeois society but deplored his unwillingness to take a political stand, and his resigned pessimism has been unfavorably compared with the progressiveness of Daumier.[3]

Busch's social criticism is recognized more clearly by attentive readers today.[4] Modern psychology has furnished the tools for a reinterpretation of some of his work.[5] The discussion of Schopenhauer's philosophical impact continues. As Kayser has shown, the grotesque element in Busch marks an important phase in the development from Raphael and Breughel to Morgenstern and Kafka. Historians of the comic strip acknowledge the importance of Busch's picture stories for this American art form.[6]

These narratives, which constitute the author's outstanding achievement, have received most of the critical attention. Busch's unique ability to tell stories in verse and drawing, with the two modes of communication complementing, emphasizing, or contradicting each other, has never been matched. In contrast, Busch's poetry is not often considered worthy of detailed analysis. Johannes Klein's decision to devote a chapter (in the section on Realism) in his history of German poetry to Busch is the exception and deserves recognition, even though some of his findings could be challenged. Few critics would agree with Walther Lampe's ranking of his poetry with that of Matthias Claudius, Eichendorff, and Goethe—despite the significant parallels in each case.[7] The more sober assessment by Heuss, who does not see Busch's poetry as a truly lyrical creation, is shared by others.[8] But perhaps in either view the standards applied are inappropriate. While it is undeniable that some of Busch's verse is imitative, and that, as Heuss asserts, much of his poetic production is owed to intellect rather than intuition, Busch is often strikingly modern in outlook and language. As a poet, especially in his satirical pieces, he provides the link between Heinrich Heine and Tucholsky, Kästner, and Biermann. The quality of his lyrical work is not uniform, to be sure, but all three collections contain numerous excellent poems that demonstrate the author's ability to "ride Pegasus unaided" and to use words just as effectively as the expressive lines of his drawings. Busch's poetry does show, however, that he was a painter at heart: abstract concepts, emotions, and moods are frequently translated into visual images.

This tendency to paint in words is evident in his prose, too. But *Eduards Traum* and *Der Schmetterling* continue to be less known and less appreciated than his other works. There are few critical studies of either book, which is all the more surprising since these two tales in many ways represent Busch's most modern writings. As Wilfried Schöller observes, the suspension of time and space and the fragmentary picture style in *Eduard Traum* point forward to Surrealist prose and the short story of the absurd.[9] The theme of alienation in an incomprehensible world that can be found in *Der Schmetterling* adds a very contemporary note to this fairy tale. Both works are important in their portrayal of Busch's society. Yet their significance as a voice for our time is perhaps even greater. That today's readers still react like Edward's listeners who prefer not to hear "things that are rather painful to the ear of a refined century" confirms Busch's judgment of his audience and attests to the timelessness of his insights.

Notes and References

Preface

1. *Jahrbuch der Wilhelm Busch Gesellschaft*, 1967, p. 56. Subsequently this publication will simply be referred to as *Jahrbuch*.

Chapter One

1. Friedrich Bohne, *Wilhelm Busch* (Zurich, 1958), p. 34.
2. Busch was familiar with *On the Origin of Species*, which was not published until 1859. He probably made a chronological error when he referred to this period in his autobiographical sketches. His major occupation with Schopenhauer fell into his Frankfort years.

Chapter Two

1. *The Grotesque in Art and Literature*, tr. U. Weisstein (Bloomington, Ind., 1963), p. 184.
2. Ibid., p. 187.
3. *Auch Einer*. Volksausgabe in einem Band (Stuttgart, 1904), p. 25.
4. Kayser, p. 188.
5. Wilhelm Busch, *Sämtliche Werke*, ed. Otto Nöldeke, 2nd ed. (Munich, 1949), 7.438.
6. "Max und Mortiz oder die boshafte Heiterkeit," *Jahrbuch*, 1964–65, p. 37.
7. See B, 1.32–34.
8. See Arthur Schopenhauer, *Sämmtliche Werke*, ed. Julius Frauenstädt, 2nd ed. (Leipzig, 1922), 6.229.
9. See Heinrich Heine, *Sämtliche Werke*, ed. Ernst Elster, 1 (Leipzig, 1887), 55 and 53–54. For a discussion of Heine's impact on Busch, see D. P. Lotze, "Buschs Jacke aus Heines Frack?" *Jahrbuch*, 1975, pp. 5–21.
10. See Heine, 2.11.
11. Responses to a questionnaire by Louise Fastenrath. Wilhelm Busch, *Sämtliche Werke*, ed. Nöldeke, 7.246.
12. *Jahrbuch*, 1961–62, p. 34.
13. Hermann Glockner, *Wilhelm Busch* (Tübingen, 1932), p. 15.
14. *Zeitgenossen*, (Munich, 1910), p. 145.
15. See *Der Witz und seine Beziehung zum Unbewußten* (Frankfort, 1958), pp. 55–56.
16. See Kayser, p. 118.

17. *Sämtliche Werke*, ed. Nöldeke, 7.433.

18. See *A Bushel of Merrythoughts* (rpt. New York, 1971), pp. 45–46. Rogers also added his poetic comments to "Hänsel und Gretel" ("Sugar-Bread") and "The Naughty Boys of Corinth."

19. Fritz, who meets with a violent end as the result of his teasing, combines the facial features of Max and Moritz. The drawing introducing him shows the same frontal view of an innocently smiling child (see 1.75).

20. *Max und Moritz*, ed. H. Arthur Klein (New York, 1962), p. 55. Brooks imitates here Busch's famous split rhyme.

21. See Wolfgang Fuchs, "Max und Moritz," *The World Encyclopedia of Comics*, ed. Maurice Horn (New York, 1976), p. 486.

22. "Wilhelm Busch," *Die großen Deutschen* (Berlin, 1957), 5.367.

23. On this, see Friedrich Bohne, *Wilhelm Busch und der Geist seiner Zeit* (Hanover, 1931), esp. pp. 34 and 41, and Peter Bonati, *Die Darstellung des Bösen im Werk Wilhelm Buschs* (Berne, 1973), esp. pp. 93–95.

24. Rudolph Wiemann suggests this rendering of Busch's onomatopoetic subtitle in his translation, *The Bees* (New York, 1974).

25. *The Bees*, pp. 30–31.

26. See Schopenhauer, *Sämmtliche Werke*, 2.153, and Joseph Ehrlich, *Wilhelm Busch der Pessimist* (Berne, 1962), esp. pp. 64–67.

27. For details on Busch's use of this source, see Otto Nöldeke, "Unserer Lieben Frauen Kalender als Quelle für den heiligen Antonius," *Jahrbuch*, 1950–51, pp. 83–89.

28. See the afterword by Moritz Jahn for the facsimile edition of *Der heilige Antonius von Padua* (*Jahrbuch*, 1953–54), p. 124.

29. Nöldeke, "Unserer Lieben Frauen Kalender," p. 88.

30. Paul Wilhelm Wenger in *Rheinischer Merkur*, July 9, 1965.

31. Edgar Alexander, "Rolf Hochhuth: Equivocal 'Deputy,'" *America*, October 12, 1963, p. 417.

32. While the trial was pending, Schauenburg published the story in his journal *Der Lahrer Hinkende Bote* as "Der hl. Fritze, genannt Sanktus Fritzonius."

33. Jahn, p. 132.

34. *Die fromme Helene* (facsimile edition, ed. Friedrich Bohne, Hanover, 1972), p. XXIII.

35. See Alexander, p. 416. H. Arthur Klein omits this passage in his translation because of its "crude anti-Semitism." See *Hypocritical Helena* (New York, 1962), p. 197.

36. For this view, see Joseph Kraus, *Wilhelm Busch* (Reinbek, 1970), pp. 127–29.

37. Quoted in Ilse Burger, "Wilhelm Busch und Otto Bassermann," *Mannheimer Hefte*, 1 (1961), p. 28.

38. When asked, "Which political trend do you like best?" Busch responded: "None" (*Sämtliche Werke*, ed. Nöldeke, 7.246).

Chapter Three

1. *A Cultural History of the Modern Age* (New York, 1954), 3.317–19. The historian Golo Mann makes the identical point in *Deutsche Geschichte des XIX. Jahrhunderts* (Frankfort, 1958), p. 457.
2. *Sämmtliche Werke*, 3.729. See also Busch, *Sämtliche Werke*, ed. Nöldeke, 8.303.
3. The expression of innocence in the accompanying drawing parallels the introductory pictures of Max and Moritz and Helena.
4. Rudolph Wiemann, in *Chip the Monkey* (New York, 1972), translates "Fipps" as "Chip," "Gripps" the cat as "Schnip," and "Schnipps" the dog as "Nip."
5. On this, see Bohne's note, in his *Wilhelm Busch*, p. 185.
6. H. Arthur Klein's translation, in *Max und Moritz*, "Ker" and "Plunk," while retaining the association with water, misses this difference.
7. R. Loring Taylor, "The Ambiguous Legacy of Wilhelm Busch," *The Great Excluded: Children's Literature*, 1 (Storrs, 1972), p. 83.
8. *Wilhelm Busch als Dichter, Künstler, Psychologe und Philosoph* (Berkeley, 1910), p. 28. But even Kraus, who stresses the ironic and satirical elements in Busch, takes this story at face value, explaining the philistine morality as the result of Busch's waning interest in the book and of his psychological and physical problems. See *Wilhelm Busch*, p. 20.
9. Kraus sees the satire here and in the introductory chapter as directed against the Munich circle of epigonic poets around Geibel and Heyse (*Wilhelm Busch*, p. 101). But the velvet barret is also reminiscent of Richard Wagner, whom Busch met in Munich.
10. *Wilhelm Busch als Dichter* (Zurich, 1967), pp. 61–62. Marxer emphasizes that Busch's aim was not to ridicule Goethe's work.
11. See Harry Steinhauer's translation, *The Sufferings of Young Werther* (New York, 1970), pp. 2–3.
12. See Kraus, p. 110.
13. Bonati discusses this gesture at length (pp. 38–43).

Chapter Four

1. *Sämmtliche Werke*, 5.492.
2. Marxer, pp. 34–37.
3. *Geschichte der deutschen Lyrik* (Wiesbaden, 1957), pp. 636–37.
4. See 100, 24–101, 22 in Lachmann's edition.
5. Johannes Klein, p. 640.
6. *Sämmtliche Werke*, 6.420.
7. Heinrich Heine, *Sämtliche Werke*, 1.117.
8. Ehrlich, p. 71.

Chapter Five

1. Erwin Ackerknecht's *Wilhelm Busch als Selbstbiograph* (Munich, 1949), analyzes the changes in the different versions.
2. See Winther, esp. p. 46.
3. *Wilhelm Busch*, p. 247.
4. For a possible source of this segment, see Dieter and Barbara Lotze, "Romanzen in vielen Dimensionen: Abbotts *Flatland* und Buschs *Eduards Traum*," *Jahrbuch*, 1976, pp. 28–35.
5. The German "Das Leben ist eine Schuld! Ich sitze sie ab!" could also mean: "Life is guilt! I am serving my time!"
6. See *Sämmtliche Werke*, 6.312–13.
7. Revelation 21 describes the heavenly city; Matthew 7:13–14 refers to the broad way and wide gate that lead to destruction, and the narrow path and strait gate of life. Henrich Kraeger points to another parallel, William Langland's *Piers Plowman* (see *Jahrbuch*, 1952, p. 22).
8. John Bunyan, *The Complete Works* (Philadelphia, 1880), p. 242.
9. Kayser, p. 119.
10. See ibid., p. 120.
11. Paul Fechter, "Anmerkungen zum 'Schmetterling,'" *Jahrbuch*, 1961–62, p. 8; Bohne, *Wilhelm Busch*, p. 263.
12. Marxer, pp. 41–60.
13. Fechter, p. 12.

Chapter Six

1. *Marx und Maoritz* (Berne, 1969).
2. Taylor's insightful essay suffers from this limited scope.
3. See Herbert Sandberg, "Größe und Grenze Wilhelm Buschs," *Dieses war der erste Streich* (Berlin, 1959), pp. 10–11.
4. See Ulrich Baer, "Wilhelm Busch als Kritiker seiner Zeit," *Jahrbuch*, 1957–58, pp. 3–11; Gert Ueding, "Wilhelm Buschs mißrat'ne Kinder," *Jahrbuch*, 1974, pp. 5–20; Wolfgang Teichmann, "Satirische Abrechnung mit der spätbürgerlichen Kultur," *Jahrbuch*, 1971, pp. 35–41.
5. Gert Sautermeister's articles in *Kindlers Literatur Lexikon* can serve as examples: "Max und Moritz," 4 (Zurich, 1968), cols. 2239–41; "Die fromme Helene," Ergänzungsband (Zurich, 1974), cols. 475–78.
6. See the references in Coulton Waugh, *The Comics* (New York, 1947); Jerry Robinson, *The Comics: An Illustrated History of Comic Strip Art* (New York, 1974); Reinhold Reitberger and Wolfgang Fuchs, *Comics: Anatomy of a Mass Medium* (Boston, 1972); Pierre Couperie et. al., *A History of the Comic Strip* (New York, 1968).
7. "Wilhelm Busch: Der Lyriker," *Jahrbuch*, 1950–51, p. 81.
8. "Wilhelm Busch," *Jahrbuch*, 1950–51, p. 6. See Gert Sautermeister,

"Kritik des Herzens," *Kindlers Literatur Lexikon*, Ergänzungsband (Zurich, 1974), cols. 636–37; Marxer, pp. 33–37.

9. "Eduards Traum," *Kindlers Literatur Lexikon*, 2 (Zurich, 1966), cols. 1836–37.

Selected Bibliography

PRIMARY SOURCES

1. Editions

Only Busch's collected works are cataloged here since the number of individual titles published in various editions, particularly after the German copyright on his works expired in 1959, is too vast to be listed. Original publication dates of his major works appear in the chronology.

Werke: Historisch-kritische Gesamtausgabe, ed. Friedrich Bohne. 4 vols. Hamburg: Standard-Verlag, 1959. Subsequent identical editions: Wiesbaden: Emil Vollmer. This is the most reliable critical edition of Busch's literary works to date.

Sämtliche Werke, ed. Otto Nöldeke. 8 vols. Munich: Braun & Schneider, 1943. Second edition, 1949. Third edition in 6 vols., 1955. A comprehensive edition, suffering from the inclusion of extraneous material and an occasional lack of critical judgment on the editor's part.

Sämtliche Werke und eine Auswahl der Skizzen und Gemälde, ed. Rolf Hochhuth. Gütersloh: Bertelsmann, 1959. Vol. 1: *Und die Moral von der Geschicht*. Vol. 2: *Was beliebt ist auch erlaubt*. A popular, uncritical edition aimed at making Busch's works accessible to a wide audience. Each volume is intended to be complete in itself. The works are not presented in chronological order.

Das Gesamtwerk des Zeichners und Dichters, ed. Hugo Werner. 6 vols. Olten: Fackel-Verlag, 1959. Despite its title, this is not a complete edition. There are significant omissions in his early work. No examples of his dramatic writings are given.

Werke, ed. Wolfgang Teichmann. Berlin: Eulenspiegel-Verlag. Vol. 1: *Dieses war der erste Streich*. 1959. Vol. 2: *Eins—zwei—drei—im Sauseschritt*. 1960. Vol. 3: *Summa Summarum*. 1961. This East German edition is not reliable in details, and the editorial comments are occasionally too one-sided in their political orientation.

2. Facsimile Editions

The Wilhelm Busch Gesellschaft in Hanover has published several facsimile editions of major works. The most important ones are:

Der heilige Antonius von Padua. 1955.

162

Fipps der Affe. 1960.
Max und Moritz. 1962.
Vierhändig. 1970.
Die fromme Helene. 1972.
Plisch und Plum. 1974 (Sixth Chapter).
Julchen. 1977.

3. Letters
All of Busch's known letters are reprinted in a critical annotated edition: *Sämtliche Briefe: Kommentierte Ausgabe*, ed. Friedrich Bohne. 2 vols. Hanover: Wilhelm-Busch-Gesellschaft, 1968–69.

4. Works in English Translation
Several of Busch's works, in particular his prose writings, have not been published in English translations. Listed below are only translations readily available in recent editions:
A Bushel of Merrythoughts. Tr. W. Harry Rogers. London: Sampson Low, Son, & Marston, 1868; rpt. New York: Dover, 1971 (includes translations of "Hänsel und Gretel," "Eispeter," "Katze und Maus," and "Diogenes und die bösen Buben von Korinth").
Hypocritical Helena Plus a Plenty of Other Pleasures. Tr. H. Arthur Klein and M. C. Klein. New York: Dover, 1962 (includes original texts and translations of *Die fromme Helene*, several picture stories from *Die Haarbeutel*, "Die kühne Müllerstochter," "Der Virtuos," and some minor pieces).
Max and Moritz With Many More Mischief-Makers More or Less Human or Approximately Animal. Tr. H. Arthur Klein et al. New York: Dover, 1962 (includes original texts and translations of *Max und Moritz*, *Plisch und Plum*, and several early shorter pieces).
Max and Moritz. Tr. H. F. Cook and F. M. Williams. London: Dent, 1969.
Max and Maurice: The Story of Two Rascals in Seven Pranks. Tr. Walter Roome. Montreal: Mansfield Book Mart, 1961.
Adventures of a Bachelor. Tr. Walter Roome. Herrenalb/Schwarzw.: Horst Erdmann Verlag, 1966.
Chip the Monkey. Tr. Rudolph Wiemann. New York: Vantage Press, 1972 (a translation of *"Fipps der Affe für Kinder"* with the pictures and some of the text of the adult edition).
The Bees: A Fairy Tale. Tr. Rudolph Wiemann. New York: Vantage Press, 1974, (*Schnurrdiburr oder die Bienen*).
Balduin Bählamm, der verhinderte Dichter / Clement Dove, the Thwarted Poet. Tr. Walter W. Arndt. Gütersloh: Sigbert Mohn, 1967 (bilingual edition).
Klecksel the Painter. Tr. Max Born. New York: Frederick Ungar, 1965 (bilingual edition).

SECONDARY SOURCES

1. Studies in English
There is very little literature on Busch in English. Some unpublished American dissertations dealing with him (Theophil Uhle, U. of Minnesota, 1951; Joseph Kraus, UCLA, 1968) and a very detailed American study of his work (Fritz Winther, 1910), were written in German.

ALEXANDER, EDGAR. "Rolf Hochhuth: Equivocal 'Deputy'." *America*, October 12, 1963, pp. 416–23. Discussion of "anti-Semitism" in Busch in order to discredit the editor of his works.

HELLER, ERICH. "Creatures of Circumstance." *Times Literary Supplement*, October 7, 1977, pp. 1124–26. A brief but perceptive appraisal of Busch's work, giving some attention to Busch's ambiguous attitude toward anti-Semitism. The article concludes with a positive review of Arndt's translation of *Bählamm*.

KAYSER, WOLFGANG. *The Grotesque in Art and Literature*. Tr. Ulrich Weisstein. Bloomington: Indiana U. Press, 1963, esp. pp. 113–21. Important insights into Busch's art, even though the investigation is limited to one aspect of his work.

KURZ, EDMUND P. "Wilhelm Busch and the Problem of Pedagogy." *Revue des Langues Vivantes*, 31 (1965), 55–61. Kurz discusses briefly the often denied influence of contemporary culture on Busch and then focuses on education and educators in his work. Busch's agreement with Schopenhauer's pessimistic assessment of the educational process is stressed.

TAYLOR, R. LORING. "The Ambiguous Legacy of Wilhelm Busch." *The Great Excluded: Children's Literature*. Vol. 1. Ed. Francelia Butler. Storrs: U. of Connecticut, 1972, pp. 77–92. Despite some questionable judgments and the unfortunate classification of Busch as a children's author, this article offers a serious discussion of his work. The second part of the essay is a partial translation of *Eduards Traum*.

2. Studies in German
The publications of the Wilhelm Busch Gesellschaft (Wilhelm Busch Society) in Hanover are indispensable to any research on Busch. They started in 1931 as *Mitteilungen der Wilhelm-Busch-Gesellschaft*, changing in 1949 to *Jahrbuch der Wilhelm-Busch-Gesellschaft* and in 1964 to *Wilhelm Busch Jahrbuch*. Articles from these publications are not included in the following selective bibliography of printed sources.

ACKERKNECHT, ERWIN. *Wilhelm Busch als Selbstbiograph*. Munich: Bassermann, 1949. A detailed analysis of Busch's autobiographical writings.

BALZER, HANS. *Nur was wir glauben, wissen wir gewiß: Der Lebensweg des lachenden Weisen*. Berlin: Evangelische Verlagsanstalt, 1954. Biography with emphasis on Busch's religious views.

BOHNE, FRIEDRICH. *Wilhelm Busch und der Geist seiner Zeit*. Hanover:

Wilhelm-Busch-Gesellschaft, 1931. This is the author's Jena dissertation. The attempt to sketch Busch's position in the cultural landscape of nineteenth-century Germany is still valid. The discussions of Busch's political works and of Schopenhauer's impact are especially pertinent.

————. *Wilhelm Busch: Leben—Werk—Schicksal.* Zurich: Fretz & Wasmuth, 1958. The definitive biography. Essential for any research on Busch. Good bibliography.

BONATI, PETER. *Die Darstellung des Bösen im Werk Wilhelm Buschs.* Berne: Francke, 1973. This study of the representation of evil in Busch's work offers many valuable insights, but the flood of details occasionally obscures the overview.

DANGERS, ROBERT. *Wilhelm Busch: Sein Leben und sein Werk.* Berlin: Klemm, 1930. Biography and evaluation of Busch's literary and artistic work. Contributed to the rediscovery of the artist.

EHRLICH, JOSEPH. *Wilhelm Busch der Pessimist: Sein Verhältnis zu Arthur Schopenhauer.* Berne: Francke, 1962. A detailed analysis of Schopenhauer's impact on Busch, sometimes losing sight of Busch's creative genius.

GLOCKNER, HERMANN. *Wilhelm Busch: Der Mensch. Der Zeichner. Der Humorist.* Tübingen: Mohr, 1932. This book grew out of a speech at Heidelberg University on the occasion of Busch's one hundredth birthday. It contributed greatly to a reevaluation of Busch's significance.

HEUSS, THEODOR. "Wilhelm Busch." *Die großen Deutschen: Deutsche Biographie.* Ed. Hermann Heimpel, Theodor Heuss, Benno Reifenberg. Vol. V. Berlin: Propyläen-Verlag, 1957, 361–67. This concise essay is one of the best discussions of Busch and his work.

HOFMILLER, JOSEF. "Wilhelm Busch." *Zeitgenossen.* Munich: Süddeutsche Monatshefte, 1910, pp. 136–81. Despite occasional hostility and some misjudgments, a remarkable early assessment.

KAYSER, WOLFGANG. *Wilhelm Buschs grotesker Humor.* Göttingen: Vandenhoeck & Ruprecht, 1958. This sixteen-page booklet grew out of a lecture on Busch and was later incorporated into Kayser's book on the grotesque. It is the best treatment of this topic.

KLEIN, JOHANNES. "Der humoristische Realismus: Wilhelm Busch." *Geschichte der deutschen Lyrik von Luther bis zum Ausgang des zweiten Weltkrieges.* Wiesbaden: Franz Steiner, 1957, pp. 632–42. Significant as the first inclusion of Busch's verse in a major history of German poetry. Some views can be questioned, but generally a positive treatment of Busch.

KRAUS, JOSEPH. *Wilhelm Busch in Selbstzeugnissen und Bilddokumenten.* Reinbek: Rowohlt, 1970. A handy and valuable monograph on Busch and his work based in part on the author's dissertation on Busch's satire. Extensive, though uncritical bibliography.

MARXER, PETER. *Wilhelm Busch als Dichter.* Zurich: Juris-Verlag, 1967. By concentrating on a few selected works, Marxer could study in depth

Busch as an autobiographer, poet, prose writer, and as the author of verse epics. Valuable insights into Busch's literary language.

PAPE, WALTER. *Wilhelm Busch.* Stuttgart: J. B. Metzler, 1977. This volume in the *Sammlung Metzler* series offers basic information about Busch, his work, and its impact. A selective critical bibliography is included.

TEICHMANN, WOLFGANG. "Wilhelm Busch heute: Zu seinem 50. Todestag am 9. Januar." *Neue deutsche Literatur* 6 (1958), 88–102. Busch's significance as seen from a Marxist position.

VOLKMANN, OTTO FELIX. *Wilhelm Busch der Poet: Seine Motive und seine Quellen.* Leipzig: Haessel, 1910. This early investigation is still valuable as one of the few attempts to trace some of Busch's sources.

WINTHER, FRITZ. *Wilhelm Busch als Dichter, Künstler, Psychologe und Philosoph.* U. of California Publications in Modern Philology, 2 (1910–1912), Berkeley: The University of California Press, 1910, 1–79. Even though this study is dated in many ways, it is significant as one of the first extensive discussions of Busch's work. Winther's attempt to relate Busch's writings to those of other authors of his century is particularly remarkable.

Index

167

DATE DUE

GAYLORD			PRINTED IN U.S.A